FIVE REASONS
CHURCHES THRIVE

FIVE REASONS CHURCHES THRIVE

A LEADERSHIP FABLE

EUGENE WILSON

WORD AFLAME PRESS
WELDON SPRING, MO

Word Aflame Press
36 Research Park Court
Weldon Spring, MO 63304
pentecostalpublishing.com

Unless otherwise identified, Scripture quotations are from the
King James Version.

Printed in the United States of America

Cover design by Jeremy Hart

32 31 30 29 28 27 26 25 24 23   1 2 3 4 5

Library of Congress Cataloging-in-Publication Data

Names: Wilson, Eugene T., author.
Title: Five reasons churches thrive : a leadership fable / by Eugene Wil-
    son.
Description: Weldon Spring, MO : Word Aflame Press, [2023] | Sum-
    mary: "This book discusses five obstacles to church growth: apathy,
    lack of diversity, restricted environment, self interest, and misalign-
    ment"-- Provided by publisher.
Identifiers: LCCN 2023009929 (print) | LCCN 2023009930 (ebook) |
    ISBN 9780757760273 (paperback) | ISBN 9780757760280 (epub)
Subjects: LCSH: Church growth--North America. | Christian leader-
    ship--North America. | Christian fiction.
Classification: LCC BV652.25 .W57 2023 (print) | LCC BV652.25
    (ebook) | DDC 254/.5097--dc23/eng/20230515
LC record available at https://lccn.loc.gov/2023009929
LC ebook record available at https://lccn.loc.gov/2023009930

THE STORY

THE APPLICATION

The Story

THE SETTING

It had been a wonderful church service full of energy from beginning to end. It was more than mere surface hype; there was a genuine move of the Lord. Several experienced the new birth, being born of the water and of the Spirit. Others were healed, and the preached Word of God encouraged many. Yet Pastor Jon Myers couldn't help but feel a little disheartened. The Pentecostals of Tri-Cities was everything he desired a church to be. The problem was . . . it wasn't his church.

The Pentecostals of Tri-Cities

The Pentecostals of Tri-Cities was pastored by Mike Chambers, a minister in his midfifties. Pastor Chambers had served as senior pastor of the Pentecostals for twenty-two years. When he assumed the pastorate, the average Sunday attendance was one hundred. It was now averaging nearly 1,100 with a membership of over 1,400. Pastor Chambers often remarked that the Pentecostals of Tri-Cities wasn't a perfect church, as there is no such thing, but God had been good.

As Jon Myers waited for Pastor Chambers to finish greeting guests, he couldn't help but wonder what he needed to do to have a church like this.

Greater Life Church

To assume that Pastor Jon faced discouragement on occasion would be accurate. Just when it appeared his church was about to turn the corner, something would happen. A leader would move away due to a job transfer. A church member would simply move membership to another church nearby without saying why. Of course, with a small-size congregation, every time someone left it was demoralizing and had a negative financial impact.

Pastor Jon, however, was convinced he was where he was supposed to be. He was unapologetic in his belief in the power of the gospel. Although he did not view himself as a conference-caliber preacher, he was given to prayer and study of the Word. He also was an effective communicator. Moreover, his leadership skills were above average. So why the challenge?

When Pastor Jon and his wife, Shelly, along with their two children, had assumed the pastorate of Greater Life Church, they had expected great things. The church was small, but that hadn't deterred them from assuming the pastorate. They were not naïve; both Jon and Shelly understood it would take some time for the church to grow, for leaders to be developed, and teams to be formed. Jon wasn't bothered by the fact that he would have to be bi-vocational for a period. What bothered him, however, and bothered him deeply, was that the number of attendees was nearly the same as it had been when he assumed the pastorate five years ago.

Despite the challenges, Jon and Shelly were committed to the church. Although it was their first pastorate, having previously served as assistant pastor, and before that as youth pastor, they felt prepared for a senior level of pastoral responsibilities.

Jon and Shelly had met at Bible college. Jon graduated with a theology degree. Shelly had quit school at the end of her junior year to prepare for their wedding. She did, however, upon getting married, continue her education, graduating with a degree in elementary education. Jon also had returned to school. While serving as youth pastor, he pursued a Master of Arts in Human Relations, a degree that had helped him get his present position in HR with a local business.

Although Jon had been a successful leader in the business, he was struggling in leading the church to grow. It wasn't for lack of effort or desire. He had attended many ministerial conferences and had read many church-growth books. He always enjoyed the conferences and derived encouragement from the preaching and time spent in fellowship with other ministers. But the excitement he felt immediately after a conference was short lived.

After one conference in which he was moved to lead the church to a deeper walk with God, he instituted early morning prayer. For several weeks only a handful of people showed up. He grew discouraged and decided it would be easier to pray at home.

There also was the time he started holding monthly leadership meetings. But after a while, that grew tiresome as well. It had been some time since he had conducted a leadership meeting. He had begun to feel the meeting was a waste of everyone's time.

Pastor Jon often pondered why it was such a struggle to translate the inspiration he felt at the conferences to the application needed at home. He did not have the answer. Although he had heard of some conferences that sought to address the practical aspect of ministry, he had yet to attend one of them. A couple of pastoral friends had, but it appeared as if they too were still struggling in applying what they had learned.

This is not to say that Greater Life Church hadn't experienced some good things. Indeed, during the first year of his pastorate quite a few good things happened. Those who had hung around the fringes of the church started attending. New people started visiting. Records from previous years showed that it had been a while since anyone had been baptized at the church and even longer since someone had received the Holy Ghost. Within a couple of months of Pastor Jon assuming the pastorate, several people were baptized and several received the gift of the Holy Spirit.

Yet despite all the good things that had occurred, there was little church growth. Perhaps most disheartening to Jon was that it seemed as if the spirit or climate of the church wasn't much different than it had been when he first arrived.

Such was the context that led Jon to approach his wife with an idea. "Shelly," he said, "there's got to be something we can do. We can't continue doing the same things and expect different results. We've talked about this before. Let's just take a Sunday and visit Pastor Chambers's church."

He continued, "We've heard about the Pentecostals of Tri-Cities. Everyone who has been there says it is a wonderful church. And by everything we've seen online, it certainly seems so. We need to experience it in person. We've got to do something."

Shelly responded, "We have nothing to lose. Let's drive over on a Saturday mid-morning and spend some time doing something fun with the kids. We can stay at a hotel."

Jon chimed in, "Maybe after service we can connect with Pastor Chambers and his wife, or one of the other staff pastors."

"I love the idea," said Shelly. "And we can certainly use the fellowship. It's been a while since we've connected with other ministers."

"We can drive back Sunday afternoon. I think they only have a 10:00 and 11:00 service," said Jon. "We should be able to eat and still leave at a decent time to make it back home so I can be ready for work and the kids can get to bed at a decent time."

And with that, they put the plan into action.

The Connection

Pastor Chambers, having previously met Pastor Jon at a conference, was quick to connect with the Myerses during the meet and greet time of the service. Upon introducing his wife to the Myerses and hearing they were in town on a short getaway, they invited them out to eat after service. Thrilled to have an opportunity to connect with the Chamberses, Jon and Shelly excitedly accepted the offer.

Once the service had ended, as they had done throughout the service, the Myerses paid special attention to things such as the culture of the church. Unlike the congregation Jon pastored, much of the church mingled together, talking and laughing, and the ministerial staff was right in the middle of it all. In addition, one minister was praying with someone and another was in deep conversation with a saint as if it were a counseling session. It was easy to see the church body was a healthy one, and Pastor Jon knew healthy things grow.

Eventually, one minister, Sam, along with his wife, Julie, approached and ask Jon and Shelly to join them in the pastor's office. Sam said, "This is where we all gather after service to decide where we are going to eat."

Jon and Shelly quickly recognized that the warmth displayed among the church members wasn't a facade; it was simply an outflow of what took place among the leaders and their families.

After the service, it seemed they waited an eternity while Pastor Chambers finished connecting with the guests who had visited. It actually was only about thirty minutes later when he finally walked into his office.

"Is anyone ready to go eat?" he asked.

All of the children immediately shouted, "Yes!" and everyone laughed.

Arriving at the restaurant, the party of fourteen were immediately seated, as someone had already called ahead for seating. After taking a few minutes to look at the menu and order some appetizers, Pastor Chambers asked, "So tell me, Pastor Myers, how are things going?"

"Things are going well," Jon replied, which wasn't entirely accurate. He added, "And you can call me Jon, or Pastor Jon. That's what everyone calls me at home."

Pastor Chambers smiled and said, "Okay, I'll call you Pastor Jon then."

It was easy to see that everyone at the table enjoyed each other's company and that the ministers of the

Pentecostals functioned as a team. It also appeared as if Pastor Chambers viewed himself as a fellow worker, although it also was easy to see that everyone highly respected him. John felt refreshed observing it all.

Later, while making the four-hour drive back home, Shelly would remark that she witnessed a similar thing while conversing with the ladies. Everyone seemed to enjoy being part of the team.

After finishing the main course, a few ordered dessert and coffee. Once again, just as it was at church, no one seemed to be in a hurry to leave. While waiting for the desserts to arrive, Pastor Chambers asked, "How long have you and your wife been serving as pastors at Greater Life Church?"

Jon remarked it had been five years and added a little insight about where they had served prior to being a senior pastor.

Pastor Chambers cracked an ever-so-slight smile and said, "Oh, I well remember the early years of our first pastorate." The other ministers chuckled, and Jon gathered that there was a story behind his remark.

Intrigued, Jon said, "I didn't know you had pastored elsewhere. And it sounds like there might be an interesting backstory."

"I don't know if it's all that interesting," said Pastor Chambers while chuckling, "but there certainly were some formative years of our ministry. We were young and full of zeal and did our best with what we knew to do. I sure wouldn't want to go back through it again, yet I wouldn't trade those times for anything."

His curiosity raised even higher, Jon said, "Please tell me about it."

"There is much to the story," said Pastor Chambers, "but here are the Cliffs Notes. We served as pastors for seven years. We thought we would be starting the church from nothing, but a few people quickly joined in. Apparently, they had been looking for someone to relaunch a church because one had closed down a few years earlier. This small group had stayed loosely connected, encouraging each other and believing God would send them a pastor. We were unaware of all of this when we decided to go. But as word got out, it wasn't long before we made a connection."

Pausing for a moment, Pastor Chambers then added, "But I'm not sure we were as much of an asset as we should have been."

"What do you mean?" asked Jon.

"Well, I guess you could sum it up by saying I didn't know what I was doing." The ministers who were sitting together at the table all chuckled.

"We struggled," continued Pastor Chambers, "but that is not to say that some good things didn't happen. For example, the church grew numerically. I guess that's a good thing. And many were saved, which is certainly a good thing. But it wasn't without its cost."

Pastor Jon said nothing, but he did wonder what the cost was.

Pastor Chambers continued, "I don't broadcast it much, and we don't have time for the entire story. Let's just say it was a trying time. Our marriage suffered, and I probably wasn't the best father I should have been."

Pastor Jon said nothing, but he and Shelly had had several conversations lately about Jon's time—or lack thereof—with the children. It was something he knew he needed to work on, but there was so much that needed to be done to grow the church.

"Eventually, we resigned," said Pastor Chambers, "and it was due to my living on the edge of burnout. I had been so consumed with growing the church that it overran my need for anything else—like my need for rest and relaxation and my need for personal growth.

"Although we grew the church to over 125 people, the cost was taxing. Many of our leaders struggled too, and we lost too many of them. I just wished I had understood then what I understand now. I think things would have been different." He seemed to be staring off in the distance.

The Challenge

Jon wasn't sure if Pastor Chambers had finished speaking, but he couldn't contain himself any longer. The openness and transparency Pastor Chambers had displayed caused him to feel safe—safe enough to share some of the struggles he and Shelley were experiencing. He spoke up. "Well, we certainly aren't anywhere near 125 people. We've been hovering around forty people. And to tell the truth, it's been quite a struggle."

Jon said nothing about his occasional bouts of burnout, nor anything about his own struggles in managing time spent with his family, nor about the battles he and Shelly had encountered in their marriage.

He continued, "I never thought it would be easy, but I certainly thought we would be further down the road than we are right now. It just seems we can't gain enough traction to get to where we need to go. We have tried many things, but getting people to stick, to stay long enough to get grounded, to get involved, to see the church grow . . . it's been quite a battle."

Pastor Chambers nodded as if he fully understood. "I know what you're saying. Don't think that everything at the Pentecostals of Tri-Cities is perfect, that everyone who comes stays, that everyone is happy and content. We have our struggles. People are people. But it is totally different now than it was during our first pastorate."

Pastor Jon was leaning forward, listening to every word. He asked, "In what ways is it different now than it was back then?"

"This might sound a little strange," remarked Pastor Chambers, "but I am less focused on growing the church and more focused on growing people. In my first pastorate I was just totally immersed with growing the church."

He's right, thought Pastor Jon. *That does sound a little strange*. While he couldn't disagree with the importance of growing people, he couldn't help but think, *Isn't it my primary job to grow the church?*

It was getting late, and Pastor Jon knew he and his family needed to get on the road. Afraid he might miss an opportunity, he said, "Pastor Chambers, thank you for inviting us to dinner today. It has been an honor to spend some time with you." Looking at the ministerial assistants who had joined them, he added, "And you guys too. I can't possibly tell you all how refreshing today has been." Then looking toward his wife, he added, "We needed this."

All who heard him remarked how thrilled they were to get to spend some time together and that they should let them know if there was anything they could do to help.

Pastor Jon smiled and said, "Well, to be honest, there is something you might be able to do."

Looking at Pastor Chambers, he added, "I actually came here today hoping I would get to spend some time with you. I know you're busy, but would it be too much to ask if I could spend some more time with you? And perhaps experience some inner workings of your church? Maybe I could even sit in on a staff meeting at some point. I've been so impressed by what you all are doing, even from a distance. And being with you today has only enhanced my curiosity. I would love to know more." With that, he paused.

"I am humbled that you would ask such a thing," remarked Pastor Chambers. "We've been blessed, and we thank God every day for what He has done. It would be an honor for me to have you look closer at what we are doing and learn the whys behind all that we do. I can't think of many things that would be more worthwhile." He paused then asked, "What might that look like considering your schedule?"

After talking it over, the two decided their get-togethers would be varied: a Tuesday staff meeting, a couple of Fridays and Saturdays, a midweek service, and at least another Sunday or two. The goal would be to meet every two to three weeks for the next several months.

Jon wasn't sure, but it appeared as though Pastor Chambers already had a plan in mind. He suggested multiple visits with different focuses were needed for Jon to come to an understanding of the whys that drove what Pastor Chambers and his church did.

Jon went out to the car excited and rejuvenated. He hadn't felt this good about their situation for quite some time. He and his wife had much to talk about.

13

INVITE OTHERS TO THE TABLE

It had been three weeks since the Myerses had visited the Pentecostals of Tri-Cities. On their way home, they had shared much with each other. Jon relayed as much as he could remember about the conversation with Pastor Chambers and the other ministers at his end of the table. Shelly informed Jon of things the ladies had discussed and added that she enjoyed the visit. It had satisfied her need for fellowship. Both agreed it had been a special weekend.

Jon also remarked that the subsequent visits with Pastor Chambers would require him taking some days off work, which meant a loss of vacation days. They willingly accepted the sacrifice, however, since they both were committed to church growth.

The real work, though, wasn't in growing a church, something they didn't fully understand at the time.

Breakfast Meeting

As Jon drove down the highway headed to his meeting with Pastor Chambers, he reflected over a few things that had occurred since his last visit to the Pentecostals of Tri-Cities.

While he and Shelly had been encouraged by the visit, upon returning home it was business as usual. It seemed the Sunday services had a little more energy, and he and his wife had purposefully sought to connect with the few guests that visited. However, it proved more difficult than it should have, as some church members sought their undivided attention. He noted it might take some time to teach the regular attendees about the importance of connecting with guests.

Jon was looking forward to his meeting with Pastor Chambers and attending Tuesday's staff meeting. Gaining some insight into the inner workings of a growing church was something he had wanted to do for a long time. Pastor Chambers had suggested that Jon drive over Monday evening, and he would take care of Jon's hotel room. He had also added that he was an early riser and would enjoy meeting for breakfast early Tuesday morning. Jon had eagerly accepted the offer.

Arriving a few minutes early, Jon thought he had beaten Pastor Chambers to the little breakfast diner where they had agreed to meet. He was wrong. Pastor Chambers was already seated. He waved Jon over.

After exchanging pleasantries and ordering breakfast, Pastor Chambers remarked, "I've been thinking about our previous conversation, and I have a few questions to ask you. Tell me, what is one of the greatest difficulties you're facing at your church, a challenge that you are struggling to overcome?"

Pastor Chambers asked this question for a couple of different reasons. One, he hoped to help Pastor Jon generate a win, something that would help the church and spark some positive momentum. Two, he wanted to gain an understanding of the baseline of Pastor Jon's philosophies or mindset. He understood that many times the struggle in overcoming growth inhibitors is rooted in how a church leader views things—their way of thinking. Although he didn't know exactly what Pastor Jon's philosophies were, he was fairly certain that some tweaking would be required. He based his assumption on the fact that he saw a younger version of himself when looking at Pastor Jon.

Jon paused before answering. Wanting to be as accurate as possible, he finally said, "I think the hurdle is largely me. I've given it lots of thought during the past few months. While I've been frustrated with the people, aggravated with their level of passion and what appears to be a lack of deep commitment, I think the biggest hurdle or challenge is me."

As Jon was speaking, Pastor Chambers mused, *This is going better than I thought. Every outstanding leader takes inventory of himself to discover what he needs to do to improve, rather than blaming others. That is exactly what Pastor Jon has done.*

To dig a little deeper, he asked, "What is it about yourself that you think is the hurdle or challenge?"

After a brief moment of consideration, Jon responded, "I think my challenge is that I have yet to communicate the vision as effectively as I should. If people caught the vision, they would follow through in doing what needs to be done. They would have the passion and zeal to make it happen." He then added with a little

17

less certainty in his voice, "I reckon I need to work on increasing my effectiveness in communicating the vision."

Pastor Chambers understood the importance of vision. It is what energizes people. The failure to transfer vision is likely the greatest contributor to the lack of follow-through. But he didn't think the challenge was Pastor Jon's lack of ability in communicating the vision. Pastor Chambers knew that transferring the vision to others comprised more than merely one person telling others the vision. The transferring of vision happens best when others are invited to share the vision.

With these thoughts in his mind, he asked Pastor Jon, "So you're telling me you believe if you could only communicate the vision more effectively, it would solve the challenges in growing your church? Is that what you're saying?"

Jon wasn't sure how to answer. *I believed that was it,* he thought to himself. *I thought the problem was my lack of ability to communicate the vision—that somehow the people weren't catching it, and that I was the problem. But even if I were to raise the bar in my ability to communicate the vision, I'm not sure that would take care of the issue.*

After a moment, he finally replied, "Now that I'm hearing what I said, I'm not entirely certain that is the issue. Even if I were to raise my level of ability in communicating the vision, I doubt it would be enough to make a difference."

As his voice trailed off, he ended by saying, "To be honest, I don't know what the problem is." Pastor Chambers laughed.

Jon wasn't sure what to think when Pastor Chambers started laughing. However, what the man said next made him feel a little better. "You are in a good place,

Pastor Jon. A better place than most people. It took me awhile to get there when I was your age. But when I did, it made an enormous difference. It wasn't long after that I experienced a major shift in my ministry. From that day forward, things changed for the better."

Jon said nothing, so Pastor Chambers explained: "When you come to the place of uncertainty, it usually means you are best poised for a change in mindset. You know that Albert Einstein is quoted as saying that the definition of insanity is doing the same thing repeatedly but expecting different results, right? I would surmise the problem is in how the vision is shared, not in how you communicate it. Sharing the vision comprises much more than you simply communicating the vision."

Before Jon could respond, Pastor Chambers asked, "What do people do when you communicate the vision?"

Jon replied, "They usually get fired up, at least that's what they did after we arrived—that is, those who were there when we arrived. As for those who started attending after we became the pastor, at first most of them seem to respond fairly well to vision. But now it seems as though it's become more difficult than ever to get people to move forward. And even more difficult to get them to stick with it. It seems the bulk of ministry is falling on just a few."

"Tell me about these people, the ones who seem to stick with things longer and help carry the load," said Pastor Chambers. "Describe to me the difference between these mighty few and everyone else."

"Well, for starters, they are more engaged. They seem to care about the church. Care about revival. Care about growth. And they do so much more than everyone else. They are more apt to respond to the

Word of God." Jon added, "To be entirely transparent, I'm not sure what all to say other than they seem to be more committed."

Pastor Chambers nodded as if he understood. He then asked, "Would it be fair to say that the mighty few have a better idea of the inner working of things?"

Jon quickly replied, "Absolutely. You can't be that involved and not have a better sense of the inner workings than those who aren't involved."

Pastor Chamber smiled as if he had just led Pastor Jon into somewhat of a discovery, but it was doubtful that Pastor Jon fully understood it at the time. He simply said, "Well then, Pastor Jon, it sounds like you might have just discovered the key to one of the growth inhibitors." Jon thought to himself, *I did?*

With that, Pastor Chambers continued, "You may not fully understand it right now, and it seems so simple—so simple, in fact, that most people fail to fully appreciate it. But the fact is, if you want to gain buy-in, invite people to sit at the table. Inviting people to sit at the table is the best way to effectively share the vision."

Jon thought, *What does he mean when he says, "Invite people to sit at the table?"*

Before he could ask, Pastor Chambers chimed in, "Time is getting away from us. We will talk more about this later. Let's head over to the church. I need to grab a few things before our staff meeting starts."

Pre-Staff Meeting

While gathering his things for the upcoming meeting, Pastor Chambers explained, "The primary purpose of our Tuesday's staff meeting is body care. We focus on things pertaining to the overall health of the church body, and there are quite a few factors involved, as you will see. We also address any issues the team members might presently be dealing with—things such as direction, advice, approval, help, and so on. While we may address other things from time to time, this is the primary purpose of Tuesday's meeting."

Having said that, Pastor Chambers continued, "It is important to note that we aren't just focusing on the body care of the congregation; we also are intent on making sure that our staff is healthy, which often includes making sure we are staying balanced, taking time for our personal relationship with God and with our family, taking time for rest, relaxation, and so on. So on Tuesdays after staff meeting wraps up, we often go out to eat together. If not, I'm usually connecting with at least one of the ministers on staff."

Pastor Chambers then broke out with a big smile, and added, "We have found that food and fellowship seem to go well together." Jon laughed.

Then Pastor Chambers quickly added, "But in all seriousness, some of our best times together—times for mentoring, times for connecting, and so on—have taken place around a table."

Staff Meeting

As the staff gathered together in the conference room, it was easy to see that everyone got along well. Besides Pastor Chambers, there were seven staff pastors and four secretaries. Pastor Chambers later explained that the targeted ratio for staffing was one full-time pastor per 150 people, and at least one secretary for approximately every 200–250 people. He also added that this was besides the multiple volunteer secretaries and admins for various ministries within the church.

After prayer and a devotional led by Pastor Chambers, the staff tackled the first item on the agenda: the attendance report. The report included Sunday's attendance with the various breakdowns of ministries such as children, youth, and so on, as well as the week before and the corresponding Sunday from last year. The attendance report also included the Wednesday night service.

This wasn't necessarily a surprise to Jon, although he admitted to himself that all they did was record the week-to-week attendance on Sunday. They did not compare it with the previous year. He made a note to do so.

What happened next especially caught Jon's attention. Bill Littles, the executive pastor who was helping to lead the staff meeting, asked Ken, the connection pastor, to review the numbers involving the connection ministry.

The connection ministry, as Pastor Chambers quickly explained, involved outreach ministry, hostesses, next steps, and other related ministries—ministries that were heavily involved in some facet of connecting guests to the church.

Pastor Ken shared how many people stopped by next steps to sign up for the membership class, a Bible study, or to join a small group. He then compared the numbers from the last four Sundays with the previous four Sundays, noting that the special emphasis placed on hostess training appeared to have had a substantial impact on an increase in numbers over the past several weeks.

Jon thought quietly to himself, *I've never seen a church be so detailed in tracking numbers like this.* It puzzled him. While one on hand the church appeared to be one big happy family that functioned primarily on organic relationships, at least behind the scenes, what he was witnessing at this staff meeting made it seem more like a business.

Thankfully, Pastor Chambers interrupted Ken's presentation as though he was aware of what Jon had been thinking. He said, "I'm sorry, but I want to take a moment to make sure Jon understands what is going on here." He turned to Jon. "We use the term 'pathway' to describe the journey we hope everyone takes here at the Pentecostals. We are intent on raising up disciple makers. This involves us equipping people to fulfill God's call on their life, to fulfill their ministry. This, of course, involves everything from giving their life to God, to fellowship, to growing spiritually, to helping people discover their ministry and getting involved in it, and so on. We use numbers to help us gauge our effectiveness in helping people along that pathway. It's not perfect by any means, but we have found it to be a great tool in helping us make sure we are giving due diligence to essential areas along the pathway to maturity." He concluded his remarks by reiterating that the Connection Ministry helps people to connect.

As the meeting resumed, Bill Littles, the executive pastor, invited Bob Cain, the growth pastor, to offer his presentation. Before Bob began speaking, Bill Littles offered a description of the Growth Ministry: "While the Connection Ministry focuses primarily on helping people to connect, the Growth Ministry focuses on helping people to grow. This includes areas such as marriage, finances, spiritual disciplines, and so on—some of which are also included in the Connection Ministry.

"The difference, however, is that the Growth Ministry is intent on tracking the growth of people. We've found it is far better to be intentional about the growth of people rather than leaving it up to chance.

"We're not interested in getting caught up in a numbers game; our use of numbers is simply to help us know where we might need to place some emphasis. If you don't measure something, you likely won't focus on it. We are very intent on helping people grow, and Bob heads up the ministry that focuses on it."

As Bob, who looked to be in his midforties, took over from there and shared his report, Jon couldn't help but think, *I can't wait until the day we can do something similar. But right now, we are way too small to do anything like all of this. And I certainly don't have the time to do anything more than what I'm doing already. So, while this is definitely impressive, it holds little value in our current context.*

As Bob concluded his remarks, Pastor Littles shifted the attention in the room to the youth pastor, saying, "Now that we've heard from both the connection and growth pastors, Pastor Tim is going to share an update on the youth staff initiative that involves both the connection and growth ministries."

Tim began his remarks by thanking the connection and growth pastors and their teams for helping the youth staff develop a process by which they were focusing on the assimilation and retention of the youth. He said, "Our youth staff, alongside the connection and growth ministries, has been working on a spiritual health project among our young people."

"Based on a criterion we have developed," he continued, "we have sought to identify the percentage of our young people who are mostly crowd people— those who are at the spiritual level of the criteria for someone who is simply part of the congregation—and the percentage of young people who meet the criteria for the committed group and core group respectively.

"We are now looking at the various events and functions of the youth ministry," said Tim, "to see if we are effectively helping those who are crowd youth to become part of the congregation, the congregation youth to become part of the committed group, and so on."

Jon understood the concept of the concentric circles; it was common knowledge among church leaders. What impressed him, however, was how the Pentecostals of Tri-Cities was applying it. He leaned forward in his seat, intent on listening closely to Pastor Tim.

"It has been a revolutionary process," Pastor Tim said. "For one thing, we realize that as the church has grown, we have become more ingrown. We need to place more focus on reaching youth. To that end, the youth staff is putting together a few youth events for this fall to be held on Thursday nights as opposed to Friday nights. The purpose of these events will be to grow the crowd, to connect youth who wouldn't typically come to a youth function on a Friday night because they typically attend high school football games."

As Tim continued sharing what he and the youth staff had been working on, Jon admired how the youth ministry had undertaken such a process and had come to such a conclusion.

For much of the remaining portion of the meeting, Jon found himself lost in thought. Each ministerial member of the team shared updates concerning objectives they and the team they led had been working on. He noticed how the team worked together, offering various opinions and thoughts. He found it all very interesting. Some team members seemed to engage more with details, while others engaged more with the big picture. Some seemed to be more people focused, and others more task-oriented. And yet the entire team worked together, helping one another, asking pertinent questions, and so on.

As Jon reflected on what he was witnessing, he mused, *I would have thought that as senior pastor, Pastor Chambers would have controlled the meeting, dictating to others various tasks that needed to be accomplished. Instead, everyone seems to be empowered.*

Jon noticed that from time to time everyone shared his or her opinion about things that were outside of his or her specific ministry. Even the secretaries appeared to be empowered, asking pertinent questions that helped shape ministry efforts. Perhaps most surprising, though, was that the ministerial leaders not only received what the secretaries had to say, they actually solicited their responses.

The Review

"Pastor Jon, what is your takeaway from the staff meeting?" asked Pastor Chambers shortly after the staff meeting had concluded.

"Well," remarked Jon, speaking slowly as if he were trying to make sure what he wanted to say, "I'm impressed with how thorough the reports were. There is much more to the numbers than I've ever seen, and to be honest, more to it than I ever thought. At Greater Life Church we're diligent in counting the number of attendees and even tracking the number of guests, but I've never considered some of those other numbers." He paused.

"What else stood out to you?" Pastor Chambers asked, failing to respond directly to Pastor Jon's new-found insight into the use of numbers at the Pentecostals of Tri-Cities.

Proceeding slowly as if he were trying to be careful in how and what he stated, Jon replied, "I was . . . somewhat surprised at how the meeting was conducted. I don't know if that is the response you're looking for or if that means much of anything."

Pastor Chambers laughed. "I'm not looking for any kind of response in particular. I'm just curious what your takeaway is. And just so you know, whatever it is, that's fine. You have nothing to worry about." Jon felt comfortable enough to join in the laughter.

Pastor Chambers continued, "When you said you were surprised by how the meeting was conducted, what exactly did you mean?"

"Well, to be honest, I thought that as the senior pastor, you would have been more in control of the meeting, directing and delegating various tasks to the team members. Instead, it appeared to be much more of a team effort with various members taking the lead—but not in a bad way," he hastily added. "I guess the best way to say it is that they seemed to be empowered. I'm not sure I've ever seen anything like it, at least not in a church setting."

Pastor Chambers smiled while remarking, "That's exactly what I was hoping you would say. You noticed something we've worked hard to create. We are intentional in empowering others: getting leaders to take the lead in building teams and empowering others. This is what I mean when I talk about inviting others to the table."

So that's what he meant when he said "invite others to the table," thought Jon. *Finally, I'm gaining some understanding of what Pastor Chambers has been talking about. Inviting others to the table has to do with empowerment instead of mere delegation.*

Pastor Chambers continued. "I grew up in a small-size church. My father was my pastor. He was a great man and an outstanding preacher. He pastored primarily in rural communities. We moved often when I was a child. Later, in my teenage years, we settled in what I now refer to as home. My parents are still living there. My father is eighty-four years old but acts like he's in his late sixties.

"Anyway, I'm getting sidetracked. When I began pastoring, I did what I had seen and experienced. Not that what I experienced as a child or did as a young pastor was wrong—I don't want you to get the wrong impression. You've done nothing wrong in your situation. You've done what you knew to do. However, there is a distinction in how I used to pastor compared to how I now pastor."

He paused for a moment and then said, "Let me ask you something. I'm assuming you and your wife probably make most of the decisions regarding the church, from everything like the color of the paint on the walls to planning a Christmas party or major event for the church. Is that correct?"

"That is correct," Jon agreed. "Not everything, but certainly most everything."

Pastor Chambers then asked, "Where do you make most of the decisions? Where are you when you're talking about such things?"

Without waiting for Jon's answer, Pastor Chambers continued, "It may not be the same as what I experienced

28

as a kid growing up at home, but when my siblings and I grew older, decisions regarding the things I just mentioned were discussed at the dinner table. We all had an opinion. That may not be the same for you, seeing that your children are quite young. But I thought I would ask to see if it there were any similarities."

Jon smiled and answered, "You're correct. Our small children make it somewhat difficult to have such conversations, consistently at least, while eating dinner. But in thinking back to our conversations before our children came along, it certainly was as you described. And I can definitely imagine it being like your experience when our children grow a little older."

Jon sighed and added, "And beyond the shadow of doubt, when my wife and I get away for a date night, we almost always talk about plans, whether it's our vacation, the children, our future, or the church. This is so interesting! I've never really stopped to consider it, but it's true; much of our planning takes place at the table."

It was what Pastor Chambers said next that really affected Jon's mindset and would, in time, influence positive changes in how he led others.

Pastor Chambers stated, "Think about this. The people in your church, people who could develop into outstanding leaders, people who could help shoulder the load—when do they, if ever, get to sit at the table and have such conversations with you? When do they ever get to sit at the table with others and carry on such conversations? Do they get to take part in meaningful dialogue, analyzing things, looking at things from various angles, getting to hear other perspectives, just as you and your wife do?"

He then interrupted himself: "You and your wife don't always agree, do you? She has an opinion that is often different from yours, right?"

Jon laughed, "You got that right."

"See, that's my point," said Pastor Chambers. "That's what I experienced as a kid. My siblings and I didn't always want to go to the same place for vacation. My sister wanted to visit metro cities. I wanted to go hiking in the Colorado mountains. Sometimes my parents would simply say, 'This is where we're going,' and we kids had little choice. But usually, our father would include us in the conversation and decision-making process. He would invite us to the table, so to speak.

"I've sought to apply the same thing at the Pentecostals of Tri-Cities. I can't imagine pastoring any other way. This is much of what you witnessed today—a team that is truly empowered to share insights, thoughts, or opinions, even if they seem to be contrary to someone else's opinion. Being invited to the table means we want to hear from you."

Jon couldn't help but think to himself, *He's right, at least in principle. Many of the decisions I make as a pastor stem from conversations with my wife, but no one else can even listen in, much less contribute anything.* He then remarked, "I get it. That's what you mean by inviting others to the table."

The Meaning of Growth Inhibitors

After returning to the hotel for a short rest and to take care of some emails and calls, Jon again met with Pastor Chambers for supper. Upon sitting down, Jon apologized for taking Pastor Chambers away from his wife. Pastor Chambers remarked, "All is well. My wife is enjoying babysitting our grandbaby tonight, freeing me up for the evening. This has worked out just right."

After ordering, Pastor Chambers said, "There's something I want to share with you. It's not anything deep, but it's something I stumbled onto some years ago that has greatly affected my thinking and, consequently, much of how I pastor.

"I'm not much of a gardener, or even a yard guy if there is such a thing. So it's probably best not to read a lot into what I'm about to say. But I am a reader. I've read about growth inhibitors in plants and found out about the various types of growth inhibitors, the most common of which is abscisic acid. Abscisic acid promotes abscission, which is what happens when a plant drops a leaf or fruit or seed. Abscisic acid promotes the development of dormancy in buds; it can even limit the size of a plant. I've realized that growth inhibitors aren't just limited to plants. People experience growth inhibitors too, as do organizations and churches.

"Think about it. Human growth inhibitors block people from reaching their full potential. The lack of self-awareness can be a growth inhibitor, and the failure not only to accept but to solicit constructive feedback also is a common growth barrier among leaders. The possibilities, I reckon, are limitless."

As he spoke, Jon thought, *That used to be me. I never would have solicited constructive feedback, but thankfully, I think I've finally moved beyond that. If not, I reckon I wouldn't be here right now.*

"Probably the most common human growth inhibitor," Pastor Chambers explained, "the thing that limits most people from being all they can be, is what goes on in their mind. Adverse childhood experiences, past failures and mistakes (and not necessarily moral mistakes), perhaps even the lack of success in life—these things and more can limit one's growth."

Continuing, Pastor Chambers referenced a comment he'd made three weeks previously, "This was one issue I myself had to overcome. Even though in our first pastorate we experienced what some would call success, it wasn't enough. So I pushed and pushed and ultimately experienced burnout. Later after some time spent recovering, God challenged me to pastor again. At first I resisted. I thought if I messed things up before, who's to say I wouldn't mess things up again? My thinking got in the way; it became a growth inhibitor.

"Unfortunately, I've seen people through the years who had enormous potential but never overcame a growth inhibitor. It stunted their growth. And you know what is especially sad?" Without waiting for an answer, he said, "Many of them were leaders. And unfortunately some were church leaders." Lowering his voice, he added, "And I used to be one of them."

After pausing for a moment, Pastor Chambers asked, "Do you know what I regret the most?" Again not waiting for an answer, he said, "I was so intent on building the church that I failed to focus on my calling to build people. I had good intentions, but I was misguided. My efforts to grow the church stunted the growth of people and ultimately stunted the growth of the church. I know it sounds like an oxymoron, doesn't it?"

Jon wasn't sure what to say; he wasn't even sure what to think. Pastor Chambers had certainly challenged his thinking, yet he wasn't totally convinced. Conflicting thoughts were erupting in his mind. *But isn't it my responsibility to grow the church? Isn't that what I am called to do?*

Pastor Chambers continued, "But that's not all. My misguided efforts on growing the church as opposed to growing people were reflected in my out-of-balance priorities with my family and my ministry. I didn't take time for my family. I didn't take time to rest as I should have. And I didn't take time to focus on personal growth outside of the drive to grow so I could grow the church numerically. You might say I was focused on 'doing,' not on 'becoming.' I didn't understand the bigger picture of what growth was all about."

Jon was at a loss for words. As the two men sat quietly, Jon admitted to himself that he'd been so focused on growing the church that he hadn't really focused on growing people—and for sure not in the way the Pentecostals of Tri-Cities did.

Finally, Jon spoke, "I teach and preach from behind the pulpit, and occasionally I counsel people, but I don't think I've ever truly sought to discover the passions, the dreams, and the desires of the people I pastor. Maybe a couple of them, but not many."

After a moment he continued, "Pastor Chambers, you've given me a lot to think about. I hear what you're saying, but I'm still trying to process it all. I must admit, it seems contrary to my way of thinking and the way I've done things."

Pastor Chambers smiled and nodded, "I understand."

Jon couldn't help but wonder how much of his present journey was like what Pastor Chambers had experienced during his first pastorate.

"Time is getting away from us," said Pastor Chambers, "and you're going to need to get on the road soon. So let me share some final thoughts concerning our time together today."

Invite Others to Sit at the Table

"I'm thrilled that you noticed I didn't dictate every-thing in the staff meeting. And I'm even more excited that you also noticed I didn't focus on delegating things. Instead, you remarked that it seemed I purposely sought to empower others.

"As I mentioned in my office, at the conclusion of the staff meeting" continued Pastor Chambers, "that is precisely what I've sought to do. Not that I never delegate things, for I do. But I would much rather empower people."

"I've never considered the difference between dele-gating and empowering," Jon said.

Pastor Chambers replied, "Well, let me attempt to explain the failure to invite others to the table. If all people do is exactly what you've assigned them to do, then they're limited in what they can contribute. And if they're limited in what they can contribute, you stand a good chance as a leader in stunting their growth. How do you think people best experience buy-in? By simply doing what they are told to do? Or by being invited to be a part of a process in which they get to create things, to fully engage their thoughts and opinions?"

Jon just nodded in agreement. The answer was obvi-ous—empowering others is better than merely dictating to others what you want done. But he had to admit he didn't empower people, at least not in the way Pastor Chambers did.

"Sadly," Pastor Chambers remarked, "in an attempt to grow the church, we have assigned tasks to people. What would happen if, instead of our trying to find a warm body to fulfill a task, we sought to help people discover their passion, their calling, and their ministry and then helped them grow into that ministry? Can you imagine what a difference that would make?"

Jon's immediate thought was, *Wow, now that is a church I would want to go to.* His second thought was, *Unfortunately, that is not the church I pastor. And that is largely because of my leadership.* He said nothing, however. He just simply nodded his head in approval.

"This is what we've sought to do at the Pentecostals of Tri-Cities," said Pastor Chambers. "We view ourselves as ministers of growth—not church growth per se, but rather growth of people. We believe that if you grow people, church growth will happen organically.

"Inviting people to the table is about helping people grow and releasing them to function in their God-given talents and abilities and callings. By allowing them to contribute—empowering people to help design and create and build and develop processes and ministries—we are removing growth inhibitors in their lives.

"Many growth inhibitors exist in people's lives. We must not be one of those inhibitors. What you experienced today isn't just limited to that specific team. Each of the leaders leads teams in which a similar dynamic occurs—inviting others to the table. And that same dynamic occurs throughout the church.

"We have developed a culture of trust—a culture that empowers people. We are intentional about overcoming growth inhibitors. The world can't stop the growth of the church. Satan can't stop the growth of the church. The church has thrived despite an array of adversity. That's why I say the biggest challenge to church growth is the growth of people."

The Conclusion

Knowing that their time together was quickly coming to a close, Pastor Chambers said, "I know you have to get on the road. Forgive me for sounding like I'm preaching. I don't mean to. But I get fired up about this. You are a great guy. It's clear you have a deep desire for growth or you wouldn't be here. Furthermore, you and your wife are deeply dedicated. You indicated you want to grow. That is why you came to visit a few weeks ago. I believe you. My question is, 'What are you doing to facilitate growth?'"

Without pausing for a response as he'd done several times before, Pastor Chambers continued, "I know you're busy. You have a job, a wife, and two small children. It isn't easy. I get it. I've been there. I know. And then there's your ministry. You preach and teach every Sunday and Wednesday. You maintain the building. Pay the bills. Try to keep everyone moving in the same direction. And then, if you're like most, you add to your already busy life this and that to generate momentum and, hopefully, growth."

Jon nodded, acknowledging that Pastor Chambers was on target.

"But your purpose, your calling," said Pastor Chambers, "isn't just to be busy. We are called to grow people, to equip them to fulfill their God-called purpose. And one way we do that is by inviting them to the table. Inviting others to the table gives credence to the fact we really care about them fulfilling their God-given ministry."

As their time together ended, Jon thanked Pastor Chambers for once again taking time to invest in his life and ministry. Although the drive home would take several hours, he was looking forward to it. Shelly would put the girls to sleep soon, so she should be able to talk for a while after he got home. He had much to tell her, especially about the idea that they needed to invite more people to the table.

REASON
NUMBER TWO

UNDERSTAND PERSONALITY TYPES

As Jon made the four-hour drive to visit with Pastor Chambers, he reflected over the past four weeks. Initially, they had scheduled to meet the previous week, but because of a death in the church Pastor Chambers had to reschedule. The delay worked well for Jon, though, as last week was a crazy week at work.

An opportunity at work had arisen in which Jon could apply what he had gleaned from Pastor Chambers on the previous trip. He mused at how one would think that a guy who worked in HR would already know the importance of inviting others to the table, but even in business, he had followed the norm of just dictating to others rather than inviting them to take part as a partner.

Jon had been assigned a task to move a project forward for his company. He and a few others had invested a significant number of hours in crafting a plan, and it was approaching launch time. Instead of launching the plan, he brought together some of the people who would be essential in making sure the project worked including secretaries.

At first the last-minute meeting seemed a little awkward. Jon shared a little of what he'd been working on so those present would have some context, and then he began asking questions. A few responded, but their answers were brief. At first the exchanges weren't as engaging as Jon had hoped for or expected, but the more questions he asked, the freer those at the table felt. It wasn't long before the team reshaped some of what Jon had worked on.

Later Jon mused that if he had moved forward without inviting the group to the table, the initiative he'd been working on would have been lacking. Much to his surprise, and thankfully so, the team came up with a better plan than he himself had crafted. Jon was thrilled at how the conversation had brought about their buy-in. Everyone was excited and ready to implement the plan the team had helped to create. It was as Pastor Chambers had said: overcoming growth inhibitors is applicable in an array of organizations, not just churches.

Driving down the highway, Jon couldn't help but wonder what he would learn during this trip. Would he be able to apply it at work too?

Going Fishing

While waiting in Pastor Chambers's office during their first visit to the Pentecostals of Tri-Cities, Jon had noticed several photos of Pastor Chambers fly-fishing. When Pastor Chambers called to plan their next meeting, he asked Jon if he would be interested in joining him for a day of fly-fishing. Jon eagerly accepted.

Jon checked into the hotel late that night and was up early the next morning. He had already eaten breakfast and was on his second cup of coffee when Pastor Chambers stopped by to pick him up at the hotel.

Pastor Chambers's love for fly-fishing was obvious. From just about the moment Jon climbed into the truck until they arrived at the river, Pastor Chambers talked almost nonstop about it.

"What do you know about fly-fishing, Pastor Jon?"

"Well, not much unfortunately. All I know is that it looks like you just whip the line back and forth."

Laughing, Pastor Chambers remarked, "I hear that often. Do you like to go fishing?"

"I always enjoyed it as a kid. But my dad wasn't much of an angler, so we didn't go often. And it was mainly with worms and a bobber. We caught a lot of small fish, as best as I can remember. When I got older, I took up golf and then got my dad into it. But ever since Shelly and I got married, I've done little of that either, other than to play a round or two with my dad once or twice a year."

Pastor Chambers said, "Well, I can't promise you we'll catch something, but I seldom get skunked. I can promise you, however, that we will have fun trying. I believe we'll catch something today, but if we don't, I know a good fish market we can stop by on our way back." He laughed.

"Oh," he continued, "I almost forgot. We're going to have supper at my house this evening. My wife is fixing an enjoyable meal. It won't be fish, though, which is one of my favorites. She's cooking a roast and potatoes with all the trimmings."

As they drove, Pastor Chambers kept up a running commentary, "You described fly-fishing as whipping the line back and forth, and I concede there's a reason for that. In fly-fishing you're using a fly that looks much like the flies that trout love to eat. It's possible to fly-fish for many varieties of fish, but my favorite is trout. The trout eat common flies of four basic groups, and those flies go through various stages of life cycle.

"Have you ever noticed birds flying over water and occasionally sweeping down to take something off the surface of the water? Those birds are eating flies that have just hatched. Once they hatch, flies only live for a short time. They mate, and then they quickly die.

"In fly-fishing, the fly should mimic whatever fly and stage of that fly the trout are eating. These flies are tied from animal hair or something similar. They weigh little if anything. In bass fishing, or when fishing with a bobber and hook, you're throwing the weight. The lure weighs enough that it can be thrown. In fly-fishing, because there's little to no weight on the fly, you're throwing a line that is weighted. That's why you see a fly fisherman going back and forth with his rod. He's throwing a weighted line."

Jon was amazed at the many details. It was bewildering. He asked, "How do you even know what to do?"

Laughing, Pastor Chambers remarked, "Well, I'm not sure any of us fishermen have all the answers. I've been fishing long enough on these waters that I know pretty well which flies to try. But that's not where you start. You always start by observing the water and how the fish are biting. The fish will tell you what type of fly to use."

It wasn't long thereafter that Jon was suited up with waders and wading boots. Pastor Chambers handed him a rod and reel and mentioned they would wait until they got to the water before tying on a fly.

Standing at the edge of the water, Jon remarked how beautiful the scenery was, to which Pastor Chambers replied, "This is one reason I love fly-fishing for trout. It's so beautiful and peaceful. I've found it is one of the easiest environments for me to hear God. I enjoy being out in nature. Besides that, as I've mentioned before, after having lived on the edge of burnout, I determined never to do that again. Hence, I never apologize for taking some time now and then to go fly-fishing."

After they had watched a few trout rise, Pastor Chambers said, "If you look carefully, you'll see a small tannish, yellow-looking fly on the water. There's one right there." He pointed at a specific spot.

About the time Jon spotted the fly, a trout rose and ate it. "Wow!" he exclaimed. "He swallowed that fly in one gulp!"

"He sure did," said Pastor Chambers. "I promise you, seeing that never gets old. Better yet, I think I know what kind of fly they're hitting on."

With that, he took out his fly box and pointed at a similar fly. "They call this a Light Cahill. My guess, from what I could see, is that we need a size 14 or 16. This is what they call 'matching the hatch'—picking out a fly that matches the real fly the trout are eating. We'll try it out and see if we have it right."

It wasn't long before Jon had landed his first trout, and on a fly rod at that. He was elated.

A couple of hours later, having worked their way down the river, Pastor Chambers stopped, took off his fly vest, and unzipped the back of it. Taking out some waters and snacks, he waited for Jon to finish fishing a run, which is a section of the river where the water is confined to a narrow current, often near the riverbank.

A few minutes later, Jon noticed that Pastor Chambers had stopped and was sitting on a log near the river. Jon waded over and joined him.

"We've been catching mostly rainbow trout," remarked Pastor Chambers, "but there are quite few brown trout in this river too. They seem to like slower water and plenty of coverage, like the shade of a tree. They're those gorgeous-looking fish with the brown dots."

"Are those the only two types of trout?"

"No, but they're the most common. If you hike up into the mountains, you can get into some brookies. They're tiny but are some of the most fun fish to catch on a fly rod. And out west you can catch cutthroat trout, which are the most beautiful of all."

Chuckling, Pastor Chambers then added, "Actually, the most beautiful trout is always the last one you catch."

The Lesson

"I asked you to go fly-fishing with me today for a few different reasons. One, I enjoy going and it's been awhile, so I was happy to get to go. Two, I love to share my passion for fly-fishing with others. I think it is one of the most peaceful, relaxing things to do."

"I like it too," said Jon. "Thanks for asking me to go. This is a blast."

"I'm glad it all worked out," remarked Pastor Chambers. "But as much as I was looking forward to sharing my love for fishing with you, I had another motive in mind. Fishing can teach us a lot about working with people. For starters, there's a lot more to fly-fishing than what we've done today. There are multiple types of flies—streamers, nymphs, midges, and so on—and different ways of fishing with them. A person can spend years learning the art of fly-fishing, only to find there's still much more to learn. Likewise, a person can spend years working with people—pastoring, leading, shepherding, and so on—and still not know it all.

"Just like what we've done today, there are some basic things that once you understand them can prove beneficial in working with people. What I mean by that is that when we started fishing today, we were able to 'match the hatch'—identify the fly that was hatching. Remember that was the fly we saw the trout eating right after we arrived at the water.

"It doesn't always work that way, though, at least not that quickly. Sometimes it's a little more of a trial and error than I would like. But the goal is still somewhat the same. If you want to catch fish, discover what they're eating.

"Likewise, a leader's success largely depends on his ability to connect with people, which requires a leader to adjust. I probably have around two hundred flies in my fly boxes here in my vest and have more boxes at home. But I can't just tie on any ole fly and catch fish. I have to use what the trout are responding to. If I use a certain kind of fly at all times, I won't have the success I desire. I have to adjust."

Jon nodded to acknowledge he was listening. It was all new and he was trying to jump ahead and figure out what this had to do with leading a church.

"It is not uncommon for trout to focus on a different fly and perhaps at a different stage of life cycle, like a nymph that's below the surface of the water. Again, if you want to have success, you have to use the fly that the trout are eating."

Pastor Chambers said while grinning from ear to ear, "Fly-fishing probably isn't the best illustration I could have used to make the point I want to make. But we will make it work anyway. A good fly fisherman knows he must adapt. It's not uncommon for me to change flies a dozen times, sometimes even more. The better my ability to know what the trout are feeding on, the better my success.

"Likewise, my success in working with people, in leading people, in ministering to people, and so on, largely depends on my ability to understand people and adjust accordingly. I've seen leaders fail as leaders because of moral failure, and I've seen leaders fail as leaders because of a wrong fit; they were trying to function outside of their gifting and/or calling. But the number-one reason leaders fail, based on personal observation, is because of their lack of ability to understand and appreciate differences in people, namely that of personality differences."

With a measure of curiosity in his tone, Pastor Chambers went on to observe, "You know, I've seen many pastors resign churches because they became weary of battling people possessed by 'evil spirits.' I'm not saying that as pastors we never deal with people who have evil spirits. I've run into them a few times myself. But more times than not, what is attributed to being an evil spirit is just differences in personalities.

"Let me say it like this: Sometimes what now is an evil spirit didn't start off being an evil spirit. It started as a lack of understanding differences in personalities and knowing how to adjust accordingly. Eventually it turned into a situation in which a person became offended. A wounded spirit that doesn't heal ends up becoming a spiritual matter. And all because of a lack of understanding differences in personalities and knowing how to adjust accordingly.

"Leaders need to know how to connect with people of all types. If a leader doesn't understand differences in personalities, he won't know how to adjust accordingly. It isn't about being a fake; it's about being wise.

"A wise leader knows how to adjust how he is communicating based on the person he's communicating with. A person's personality will tell the leader to either use stories or to get straight to the point. It will tell the leader to either share details or to focus on how a person is feeling. A highly effective leader understands he has to adjust accordingly."

His eyes darting to the stream, Pastor Chambers excitedly exclaimed, "Did you see that trout rise over there?" He pointed to a run in the river. "If I'm not mistaken, it just took a caddis fly. Typically, you can easily distinguish a caddis fly from other flies by the way it flies, which is very erratic. Nothing graceful about a caddis fly at all. But they're a lot of fun to fish with. We should probably tie one on. I think it was a size 12 Elk Hair." And with that, he opened his box to find it.

While changing flies, he continued, "Just as we are changing flies due to what we observe taking place on the water, a leader must adjust his approach based on personalities."

After a few minutes Pastor Chambers said with excitement, "Oh man, they're really going after those caddis flies. Let's continue this conversation at supper. For now, let's go catch some more trout as we work our way back up the river."

With that, both men arose and got back to fishing. Over the course of the next couple hours, both men caught quite a few trout. They changed flies a few times, as the caddis hatch eventually died off, and it took a few changes in flies before Pastor Chambers found success using a Blue Wing Olive. They both tied one on.

Finally, Pastor Chambers stopped fishing and motioned for Jon to catch up. When he did, Pastor Chambers said, "This is always the most difficult part of the day—leaving while the trout are still rising. But I told June we'd be at the house no later than 6:30 for supper. We better call it a day and get on the road."

Fellowship with the Chambers Family

When they had finished a delicious meal of roast and potatoes with all the trimmings, June brought out an apple pie and ice cream for dessert. After having spent the day on the river, Jon had come to the table hungry. He commented about that and added, "Now I'm leaving stuffed." The Chamberses both laughed.

Picking up their coffee cups, Pastor Chambers and Jon made their way to the living room to continue their conversation. Ensconced in easy chairs, both men reflected over the day of fishing and the wonderful meal. Jon then added, "And not only was it a great day for fishing, but you really got me thinking about some things when you were sharing the similarities between fly-fishing and working with people."

Pastor Chambers chuckled and said, "Well, I did my best to make the analogy work. I hope it made some sense to you."

"It definitely did," replied Jon. "You said one thing in particular that I've been mulling over in my mind, something to the effect that the greatest leadership failure you've seen is the lack of ability to recognize differences in personalities. I don't want to be that guy, but I probably have been that guy." Jon laughed to lighten his admission. "Now I have a question. How do I recognize differences in personalities?"

"There are various personality models," said Pastor Chambers. "The model I'm fond of is the DISC model. The basics are that people usually are gifted either in seeing the big picture or in seeing the details, and they either are people-oriented or task-oriented.

"In the DISC model, the D stands for Dominant Driver. The Dominant Driver is a big-picture, task-oriented person. Such a person is decisive, competitive, strong-willed, driving, determined, logical, and independent. Dominant Drivers place chief value on time, challenge status quo, are problem solvers and risk takers, and are good at making quick decisions."

"Sounds like one of my close friends," remarked Jon. "He can be quite annoying," he added as he began smiling, "especially when he doesn't want to listen to anyone else."

"I know people like that too," said Pastor Chambers. "In fact, they have accused me of being that very person. I have a lot of Dominant Driver tendencies." He laughed. "The I in the DISC model stands for Inspiring Influencer. An Inspiring Influencer is a big-picture, people-oriented person. Such a person is sociable, optimistic, talkative, enthusiastic, persuasive, warm, trusting, and independent. Inspiring Influencers are creative problem solvers, great at motivating others, possess a positive sense of humor, are good at negotiating conflict, and have great storytelling abilities. Do you know of someone who might be an Inspiring Influencer?" asked Pastor Chambers.

"I think I do," remarked Jon. "The description of an Inspiring Influencer sounds a lot like me."

Chuckling, Pastor Chambers said, "I thought so. That's why I asked. People like you are the life of the party. You bring a lot of passion and energy to things and have tremendous people skills. I need people like you in my life. I will miss out on caring for people if I don't have people like you around me.

"Let's talk about people who display the traits of a Steady Supporter (S). A Steady Supporter is a detail- and people-oriented person. Such a person is often shy, conservative, loyal, cooperative, predictable, deliberate, reflective, patient, caring, and kind. They are loyal team workers who can consistently do the same job, which isn't like you and me at all," said Pastor Chambers. Jon agreed.

"Secure, non-threatening surroundings are important to Steady Supporters. They are patient and relaxed and are content to hang back in the crowd and look for direction from others. Steady Supports make great team members. And we need lots of them. Interestingly, they make up the largest percentage of the population.

"Somewhat like Steady Supporters, Cautious Contemplators (the C in the DISC model) are detail people. But unlike Steady Supporters, who are people-oriented, Cautious Contemplators are task-oriented people. Words that describe Cautious Contemplators are correct, calculating, cautious, introspective, proper, follows the plan, systematic, critical, careful, organized, deep, guarded, reflective, orderly, and faithful.

"They are logical and analytical. They like instructions, rules, and policies. They tend not to care as much about the feelings of others as they do getting things right. Cautious Contemplators prefer quality and reject phoniness in others. They are motivated by explanations and projects that stimulate their thinking. Such people make great bookkeepers or accountants, but that is not to say we should limit them in those roles. It is simply to say that Cautious Contemplators go by the book."

Jon responded, "Wow. That gives some definition to things. Sounds like my wife is largely a Cautious Contemplator. I can see how our differences in personalities have affected our relationship."

"How is that?" asked Pastor Chambers.

"Well, for one thing, my wife sometimes asks questions that make no sense to me. I give a brief answer that apparently isn't detailed enough, so she then asks another question. I don't know what she's trying to get at or seeking to understand. If I'm not careful, I will start telling her everything I can think of regarding what she is asking, thinking that if I say everything I know, she won't ask me any more questions. When I get done, she often responds with 'I didn't need to know all of that. I just needed to know _____.' You can fill in the blank with whatever," said Jon, laughing. "My point is, I guess sometimes I appear to her as being too *out there*, with no details and all vision. To me, my wife sometimes is *too* detail oriented. I'm seeing more clearly now than ever before that neither of us is wrong nor right. It's just differences of personality."

"That's it exactly," said Pastor Chambers. "Now think about your church. It is composed of people who are Dominant Drivers, Inspiring Influencers, Steady Supporters, and Cautious Contemplators. Some people are big picture and are neither good at nor enjoy dealing with details. Some are people-oriented and care little for tasks, whereas others are task-oriented and would prefer using people to accomplish tasks.

"And let me add, there is nothing wrong with that. It is what makes Dominant Drivers who they are. Not that they don't care for people; it's just that they're task-oriented. They're about getting stuff done. On the other hand, if things are left entirely up to Inspiring Influencers, not much will get done. But they won't care as long as everyone is having fun!" Pastor Chambers's chuckle was contagious, and Jon laughed.

"So true," said Jon. "I get it. I love to have fun, but it can be detrimental. I can get so caught up in the moment—loving the big picture and the vision aspect of things—that I don't think through the details that are involved. I've never really considered it before, at least not in these terms, but this really helps me. It makes me appreciate the differences in personalities. And most important, it gives me some understanding of how to work with people."

"I'm glad you think so," said Pastor Chambers. "But the subject is much bigger than what you probably think."

Evangelism and More

"Consider this," said Pastor Chambers. "A robust understanding of differences in personalities can prove beneficial when giving an altar call, when praying with someone in the altar, when helping someone deal with grief, when dealing with conflict, and so on."

Uh-oh, thought Jon. *Has my lack of understanding personality differences been a growth inhibitor?*

Continuing, Pastor Chambers said, "Consider how a pastor's personality influences his approach to evangelism. For example, a Dominant Driver will present the gospel straightforwardly, which calls for listeners to choose a response between Heaven or Hell. Of course,

I'm being a little dramatic, but at the core, a Dominant Driver drives people to decide.

"If a pastor is an Inspiring Influencer, much like you, his approach will be to appeal to people with a message that goes somewhat like this: 'Give your life to Jesus and He will give you joy, peace, and life more abundantly.' A pastor who is an Inspiring Influencer will be prone to host block parties, have fun, and use such things to attract people to the church."

Jon started laughing. "Yep, there's no doubt about it. I'm an Inspiring Influencer. I'm always talking about life more abundantly. We even renamed the church shortly after we arrived—Greater Life Church. Wow, I didn't know my personality had anything to do with that, but I reckon it did. I can't wait to tell Shelly. She's going to be blown away!"

Jon then asked, "So what is the approach to evangelism for a Steady Supporter? No, wait—let me guess first. A Steady Supporter is a people-oriented person who likes details. You described them as shy, caring, and kind. You also said they like secure, non-threatening surroundings. So my guess is that they would like to get to know someone, to develop a friendship with them first so they can present the gospel in a non-threatening manner. Am I correct?"

Laughing, Pastor Chambers said, "Yes. Steady Supporters are most likely to bake a cake and take it over to their neighbors, hoping to build a good relationship before they ever consider sharing the gospel message. They truly believe that no one cares to know what you think until they know you care. What about Cautious Contemplators? Do you want to guess their approach to evangelism?"

Jon said, "I was just giving that some thought. My wife is a Cautious Contemplator, but I'm not really sure what her approach to evangelism is. She is all over the board, at least it seems so."

"You've made an interesting observation," remarked Pastor Chambers. "This is something I meant to mention earlier. Just because a person's personality would lean a particular direction doesn't mean they can't step outside of the norms. Many times, we function from learned behavior rather than our truest personality. This doesn't negate, however, the benefit of understanding personality differences. Cautious Contemplators are deep thinkers, analytical types who look for answers. Hence, with evangelism, they want to answer questions by giving accurate information. There's nothing superficial about Cautious Contemplators. They don't have an abundance of close friendships, but the ones they have are very close."

"Oh my," remarked Jon. "You've described my wife to a T. There's nothing superficial about her."

Pastor Chambers leaned back in his chair and smiled as Jon shook his head in amazement. Jon finally spoke: "I never would have imagined all of this, and from a simple understanding of personality differences. And if you think that's something, there's more," said Pastor Chambers. "Your congregation, as I mentioned earlier, comprises people from all personality traits. Thus, if you're preaching from your personality trait only, let's say as a Dominant Driver, then you'll come across as being very direct, opinionated, unwavering, demanding, and challenging. There's absolutely nothing wrong with any of that; however, you would be wise to recognize that you may struggle in connecting with a Steady

Supporter who isn't direct, who doesn't like confrontation, and who struggles with confrontation.

"Or consider the Cautious Contemplators who need answers to their questions. They are task-oriented like the Dominant Driver but need details. And the Dominant Driver is a big-picture person. If the Dominant Driver preacher doesn't offer details, they're going to struggle in connecting with Cautious Contemplators, at least in that regard. And the same is true for Steady Supporters who also are detailed oriented.

"The point is, regardless of your personality type, there are people in your audience who are D's and I's and S's and C's. If you're speaking primarily from your personality, you've failed to connect or appeal to three-quarters of the congregation.

"But it goes beyond that. If you fail to understand and appreciate the differences, you won't connect and ultimately will not lead properly. And in time, some people, good people, will move elsewhere.

"I learned this through experience," said Pastor Chambers. "From time to time through the years, especially in my first pastorate, good people would leave . . . just start attending church elsewhere, never really stating why. Oh, they would give me a reason, but the reasons never really made sense; that is, until I was introduced to differences in personalities.

"Many of them were Steady Supporters. Such people don't like to deal with conflict. They thrive on being able to offer support to a vision, to a big and important cause. But as a Dominant Driver, I failed to consider their need for time with their families and time to rest, and I also failed to show simple appreciation for their labor. I didn't do this intentionally, mind you. I cared about them. But the vision or the task in fulfilling the vision was definitely my priority. And they knew it. After a while, they grew tired of my constant jumping from one thing to another. Unable to keep up, they eventually moved on elsewhere.

"I'll say it again: You have to be willing to adjust. And it is the person you are dealing with that determines the best approach."

The Pathway to Ministry

Jon sat silently, spellbound by all Pastor Chambers had just shared. He had been aware of personality differences and even had some understanding of different personality assessments, but he had never considered how impactful it was with ministry. It blew him away.

After a moment of silence, Pastor Chambers continued, "There is so much application to all of this. For example, at the Pentecostals of Tri-Cities, we use the DISC personality model as part of our pathway to ministry. We have Discover Your Ministry classes in which we teach the DISC model.

"By the end of this series of classes, each participant will have taken the personality assessment. Our secretaries enter the results into our membership database for future reference, and we follow up with each student with a personal consultation in which we help navigate them to meaningful ministry, something that fits their passion, calling, talents, and personality.

"While anyone can get involved in serving in some capacity, if a person wants to get involved in leadership, he or she must take the DISC personality assessment. We want to do our best at making sure we work together as a team as effectively as possible, and understanding personality differences is a large part of that aim."

"Wow! I wished I'd known all of this before I started pastoring. I can already see where it would have benefited me greatly," said Jon. "What got you started in all of this?"

"Years ago," said Pastor Chambers, "in my first pastorate, I found myself frustrated with some of our leaders. Basically they weren't doing things the way I would do them, so I did my best to train them. One day I realized I was trying to make my assistant just like me, when in actuality, he was much like my wife. I didn't need my wife to be like me; I needed her to be her. She completed me. It took me a few years into our marriage to celebrate our differences as opposed to trying to make her like me.

"The same thing happened with my assistant. When I realized I was doing the same thing I had done early in my marriage—trying to make him like me—I stopped. Instead, I started celebrating our differences. It was liberating.

"I didn't understand the differences in personalities then. I knew nothing about the DISC personality model or any of the other various personality models like colors, Myers-Briggs, and so on. But now I have a greater understanding and appreciation."

Pastor Chambers said with emphasis, "And that, my friend, is one of the greatest points I can make concerning the importance in understanding personality differences—we need to appreciate people for who they are. Most people desire to grow, but they want to be valued for who they are. They don't want to constantly be *fixed*, so to speak. They don't want to be made to fit into a certain mold, into the mold that is based on your personality."

The Wrap-Up

During Pastor Chambers's monologue Jon grew deeply reflective. When the older minister paused, John added, "That probably explains the resistance I have felt from some."

"What is that?" asked Pastor Chambers.

"I've been frustrated at what I have perceived to be a lack of response in praise and worship. I've been wanting some people to get with it, but by 'getting with it' I've been wanting them to respond as I would, based largely on my personality. I find myself wanting them to respond as an Inspiring Influencer might respond. Instead, some are responding much like my wife, a Cautious Contemplator. I've been reading them wrong and thought some of them were resisting my leadership. But that's not the case at all. I'm just failing to understand their personality."

Pastor Chambers nodded encouragingly as Jon continued, "I get it now. For some, the raising of their hands and a tear in their eye is on a par with an Inspiring Influencer dancing and shouting."

Pastor Chambers acknowledged, "It took me years before I understood that. It's much like fly-fishing, isn't it? If you don't adjust, your chances of success will be diminished. Earlier today I mentioned that the lack of understanding differences in personalities is the number-one reason for leadership failure. I really do believe that, and I've witnessed it repeatedly. Unfortunately, we often create issues where no issues would have been. Or we take situations that could have been dealt with and turn them into a major blowup because we lack the proper understanding of how to work with people.

"I know what the common thinking is. We don't say it like this, but the normal thought process is 'I'm the pastor, and people just need to do what I tell them to do. If they don't, then they have something wrong with their spirit.' But that's wrong. Our lack of understanding how to work with people causes issues that then turn into opportunities for offense, which can lead to rebellion. I've seen it happen.

"Our lack of understanding differences in personalities, in truly appreciating one another, in working together as a team and giving honor to one another is a growth inhibitor. It must be overcome if you want to lead a church that thrives."

Pastor Chambers stood up and stretched. "Well, it's been a full day. Tomorrow is Saturday, and we have much to prepare for. I had originally planned on meeting up for breakfast before you head out of town, but if you don't mind, I think we'll wait on that for another trip. Out on the river today, God spoke something to me for Sunday that I wasn't intending on speaking about. I need to spend a little time tomorrow in prayer and study."

Jon nodded his head in acknowledgment, and added, "I certainly understand, and I need to spend some time in prayer and study too. If I get up early, I should be able to get most of it together before leaving the hotel. That way when I get home, I can enjoy most of the afternoon with the kids."

Hearing that the conversation was ending, June met them at the front door and invited with a smile, "Next time please bring your wife."

As Jon headed to his hotel, he thought, *Pastor Chambers never said what June's personality type was, but by what I've witnessed, I would surmise she is a Steady Supporter. If so, she and my wife will get along very well, at least in relationship to details.*

EXPAND THE STRUCTURE FOR GROWTH

It was a little frantic the morning Jon and Shelly pulled out of the driveway on their way to visit with Pastor Chambers and his wife, June.

The original plan was to leave Friday evening when Jon got off work, But some things arose at work that kept him there longer than he expected. Then on the way home he received a call from a couple who had recently started attending church. They were having marital difficulties and needed to talk.

Normally Jon would have postponed the meeting until Sunday afternoon. But since he and Shelly were planning on being at the Pentecostals of Tri-Cities on Sunday, Jon decided to meet right away. He hoped there would still be enough time afterward to make the four-hour drive, but it wasn't to be. By the time he finished the counseling session, it was too late to leave town.

When he called Shelly to tell her he had decided to meet with the couple, she wasn't too pleased. She understood the situation, but it was messing up their plans. After all, as she noted, she and Jon and been so busy during the past several weeks that they hadn't had any alone time. Jon choosing to counsel this new couple meant they would have to forgo their date night and postpone the plan to stop about halfway on the drive to eat supper at one of their favorite steakhouses.

Shelly's parents had come over to watch the children, and, after they woke from their naps, they planned to take them to their house. Jon's late counseling session meant Shelly's parents could return home but would have to rise very early the next morning and come to take the children to their house. In Shelly's mind, Jon's lack of awareness of the entire matter was infringing upon everyone. All he cared about was others; he didn't care about his own family.

Of course, Shelly knew that wasn't true, but that's how the circumstances made her feel. She had expressed her displeasure with the situation, and Jon had responded somewhat irritably. Now that they were finally underway, the atmosphere in the car was somewhat strained.

Jon was thinking, *Shelly is being unreasonable about all of this. Her mom and dad are early risers, so coming over early on a Saturday morning wasn't that big of a sacrifice for them. Shelly's probably right, though; the counseling session probably could have waited until the following week. The couple's marriage didn't get in the state it is in overnight, and it certainly wasn't going to get to where it needed to be with one counseling session. But why does my wife have to be so rigid? Why can't she be like me and go with the flow?*

A while later, while thinking about his upcoming visit with Pastor Chambers and wishing they were going fly-fishing, he remembered something Pastor Chambers had said, at least in so many words: "If you want to be successful as a leader, you must be willing to adjust." *Isn't that exactly what Shelly should do?* Jon thought. *She needs to adjust to the situation.*

Then he mused, *But that isn't really what Pastor Chambers was saying. He said that as a leader, I need to adjust my approach. I should not require others to adjust their approach for me; I should adjust for them. Shelly is a Cautious Contemplator. Didn't Pastor Chambers say that Cautious Contemplators follow the plan?*

The more Jon thought about it, the more his understanding grew and his irritation with the "way Shelly was acting" declined. She wasn't trying to be difficult. Her personality was to be organized. He had changed the plans without asking her to be a part of the decision process.

Oh my, he thought. *This might take more work than I imagined. I failed to invite Shelly to the table, and I failed to consider her personality. My goodness, it's one thing to understand the value of a principle, but it's quite another thing to apply it, to live it out in the moment as opposed to doing what you've always done.*

It was a milestone moment in Jon's journey in overcoming growth inhibitors. Jon decided right then and there that he would do more than simply seek to understand the growth inhibitors; he would truly seek to change. He was determined to do more than just acquire head knowledge.

"Shelly," he began, "I'm sorry. I think I just violated what I've been learning from my visits with Pastor Chambers. First, I failed to invite you to the table. That is, I didn't even ask for your thoughts regarding me changing our plans. Nor did I consider how I was messing up the plans you had organized with your mom and dad watching the kids, our dinner plans, and so on."

Shelly said, somewhat mollified, "Well, just so you know, it did aggravate me. I mean, not that you counseled the couple. If you felt that was what you needed to do, I would understand. It's just that you considered nothing else. And I was right; by your own admission just now, you considered nothing else. Having said that, I forgive you.

Jon smiled. *There it is again,* he thought. *Her personality is shining through—critical thinker, analytical, motivated by explanations. I think I will leave it all alone and just appreciate her for who God made her to be. She's an amazing woman. I'm blessed to have her by my side.* And with that, he reached over to hold her hand.

Saturday Afternoon Talk

While traveling down the road, Pastor Chambers called to let them know that something had come up unexpectedly, and he and June couldn't meet with them for lunch as planned. Instead, they would meet for coffee around 2:00 in the afternoon.

He also suggested they try one of his favorite places to eat—a place outside of the city near the river where they had gone fly-fishing. It was a quaint place with outstanding food and atmosphere—you could eat outside overlooking the river.

Jon and Shelly decided the restaurant was everything Pastor Chambers described and more. They enjoyed their meal immensely. Shelly said with a smile, "It's amazing how all of this has turned out. I was disappointed that we didn't go out last night, but I'm loving this place."

After their meal, the Myerses made their way to a coffeehouse in a small community nearby. It too was a quaint place. The Chamberses weren't expected to arrive for about thirty minutes, so Jon and Shelly walked around town, in an out of shops. It was so relaxing and restful. All the struggles from the evening before and the morning seemed to dissipate.

As they were headed back to the coffeehouse, they noticed the Chamberses getting out of their car. They waved and waited for them. Soon they were all seated, smiling, and talking about how beautiful the little community was. Pastor Chambers mentioned it was one of their favorite places to spend a day and, evidently, by the expression on June's face, he wasn't alone.

Pastor Chambers asked, "What did you think about Ben's Place, the restaurant on the water?"

"We loved it!" said Shelly. "The food was outstanding, and the service was great too."

"I'm glad you liked it," said June. "It is one of my favorites."

"Did you notice the coffee house says Mary's Place?" asked Pastor Chambers.

"What?" said Jon. "I only noticed that the sign said, 'Coffeehouse.'"

"I noticed it," said Shelly. "It says, 'Coffeehouse' and then right below that it says, 'Mary's Place.' Are the two restaurants connected?"

"Yes," said June. "Ben is the husband and Mary is his wife."

Laughing, Jon asked, "So, did they have a fight and decide to do their own thing?"

"No. But there's an interesting story behind it all," Pastor Chambers replied. "It all started as a food truck in the city."

"What?" remarked Jon and Shelly at the same time.

"Yes, amazing, isn't it?" said Pastor Chambers. "Their business flourished in the city, but they both love the country. After having saved up some money, they were able to buy the land on the river. It wasn't long before Ben constructed a small building and opened his restaurant. But once it opened, much like the food truck, the business took off. It wasn't long before they had as many customers as they could handle.

"About two years after opening, Ben built an addition to the building, along with the large deck. A couple of years later, there was another addition to the building, partly to increase the size of the kitchen and some additional dining and an expansion of the bathrooms.

"I don't recall when Mary opened her place, but it was sometime between the second or third additions to the restaurant."

June said, "Mary's story is interesting too. She opened her place because she loves coffee. It wasn't long before she started traveling to various places looking for the perfect coffee bean. She has become quite the expert. From what we heard recently they now own a coffee bean farm somewhere—I'm not sure in what country. It's all very amazing. And as my husband said, 'It all started with a food truck.'"

"Well," chuckled Pastor Chambers, "I reckon now is a good time to let you know that Ben and Mary's story is the object lesson for the third growth inhibitor I was planning on sharing with you."

June started laughing, and when she did, Jon and Shelly joined in.

Jon mused, "You're quite the expert with object lessons, Pastor Chambers. Last time, it was fly-fishing. This time, it's coffee."

"Well, it isn't coffee to be exact," remarked Pastor Chambers. "Rather how Ben and Mary went from a food truck to a growing restaurant and a coffee business that is now shipping coffee around the nation."

The Lesson

Pastor Chambers continued, "When Ben got started, he was managing a warehouse. He would operate his food truck on Friday evenings and Saturdays. The warehouse wasn't super large, but he had five to six employees. In order to open the food truck, he started working ten-hour days at the warehouse so he could take half the day off on Fridays.

"It wasn't long before the food truck was doing great. Ben then saw an opportunity to expand hours and add additional nights. But the business wasn't large enough at the time to replace his income with managing the warehouse, so Mary went to work at a coffee shop." Pastor Chambers chuckled.

Jon laughed. "So that's where she got started."

"That's right," said Pastor Chambers. "Mary's finding employment enabled Ben to quit his job managing the warehouse. It wasn't long before his food truck business exploded in growth. Mary soon quit her job at the coffee shop in order to help him run the food truck.

"Within a few years they had saved enough money (I think there might have been a partner who helped them) to purchase the land and build the first phase of Ben's Place. When Ben's Place opened, the growth was slow at first. It took a bit of time for people to find out about it. Also, this little community was undergoing some revitalization, improving roads, changing out some lights downtown, and so on.

"It wasn't long before it all came together, however. The folks in the city started coming in larger and larger numbers, and the word spread concerning Ben's

Place. And, of course, the people who had frequented the food truck came too. They were avid fans of Ben's food, and now with an expanded menu, they were eager to try it out and loved it.

"Of course, there is one other factor: Ben is an Inspiring Influencer. Everyone he meets loves him. The guy doesn't know a stranger." Pastor Chambers paused to emphasize his next statement. "At one point Ben almost lost it all—his health and his family."

Jon was shocked. "What happened?"

"It was after the second expansion and his business was growing. Now the restaurant had more dining space and a large deck had been added. On top of all that, Mary had recently launched Mary's Place and was traveling, looking for the perfect coffee bean."

"Oh," Jon remarked, "I guess they both were too busy."

"That's part of the issue," replied Pastor Chambers, "but not all of it. Ben was overwhelmed. He was working more than eighty hours per week. He needed a team, others he could turn things over to. Not that he didn't hire employees. He did. But he wouldn't let go of things, and after a while it got to be too much for him."

Jon said, "Let me make sure I'm understanding you correctly. Ben hired people to help him, but he wouldn't let go of things. So what did the employees do? Just stand around and watch?"

"No. That's not entirely it," said Pastor Chambers. "The employees all had tasks, but everyone got their daily 'marching orders' so to speak from Ben. And even if they knew what to do, they still went to Ben on getting direction for things that Ben should have been empowering them to handle on their own.

"This is what Ben told me one evening: 'Our business has grown,' he said, 'but I haven't grown with it.' And then he told me that he had become the lid to the additional growth of the business. And it was during all of this that he almost lost it—even his mind. The stress of trying to do too much just about killed him. He ended up in the hospital with chest pains, thinking he was having a heart attack. He wasn't, thankfully. But he felt like it. He said it was a wake-up call. The doctors told him he needed to make some lifestyle changes or the next time it could be the real thing."

Jon remarked, "So to a certain extent, this sounds closely related to the first growth inhibitor—not inviting others to the table."

"It is, yet it's a little different. Inviting others to the table is about allowing others to have a voice. The growth inhibitor I'm sharing with you now has to do with the structure of an organization. Leaders become the lids to growth when they cannot allow the structure to change.

"This is what Ben was doing. His business had grown, but he was still functioning as if it were a food truck. Instead of it being just him and maybe a couple of others, he now had many 'others'—servers and hostesses and cooks and cleaning people and more. At first, he could manage it. He had enough common sense to hire people to do those things, but—and here is the challenge—he thought he had to be involved in all of those things. He wouldn't turn loose of any of the oversight of the functions. And as he added more to his plate—ordering supplies, the building additions, and so on—it all became overwhelming."

"Wow!" said Jon. "I can see what you're saying. I have a question, though. How do you know so much about Ben's story?"

Pastor Chambers laughed. "You should have asked me why Ben's Place is on the river," he said. "Ben is my fishing buddy. He loves to fly-fish but never had the time. He thought being by the river might give him some time here and there to step into the water. It didn't though. He was too busy. That is, until he made some changes. And I was instrumental in the process, since I had traveled a similar path."

"What?" exclaimed Jon.

"I haven't shared with you all the lessons I learned during my first pastorate," said Pastor Chambers. "One of those lessons was that structure must change as an organization grows. Every organization undergoes stages of life cycles. In order to transition to the next stage, a leadership crisis must first be properly addressed. Leaders must adjust to a growing organization. Leaders must grow, or they will become the lid that stifles the growth of an organization.

Pastor Chambers sighed and concluded, "I know you all left very early this morning. Why don't you go check into your hotel and take some time to rest? Let's meet up around 6:30 this evening for supper. I want to take you all out to our favorite steakhouse." Shelly couldn't help but smile.

Structure Changes

The steakhouse was every bit as good as the Chamberses had promised. The food was even better than the steakhouse the Myerses had passed up due to Jon's decision to counsel the couple after work on Friday.

Later Shelly told Jon so and remarked that it had all worked out well.

While waiting on dessert, Pastor Chambers said, "Pastor Jon, I want to pick up where we left off at the coffeehouse earlier today. I was saying that organizational structure must grow as an organization grows. But in order for it to grow, leaders must first address the leadership crisis. Here's a little more to the story concerning my connection to Ben.

"I learned Ben liked fly-fishing while picking up some carryout one day. He noticed my fishing clothes and asked if I'd been out on the river. When I told him I had, he informed me he had purchased his place on the river partly because he was hoping to have time to fish here and there.

"His business, however, had grown so quickly and his responsibilities had increased to the extent he had no time at all to go fly-fishing. Of course, I encouraged him to take time, but he wouldn't listen. He eventually developed health issues. I stopped in one day a few weeks after his health scare. He was still shaken up over it. He knew I was a pastor, and he asked me to keep him in prayer. The entire matter forged a relationship. He and Mary have even visited our services a few times.

"The more Ben and I talked, the more I realized his experiences paralleled mine. For instance, during the craziness of our first pastorate, I had an anxiety attack. Like Ben, I thought I was experiencing a heart attack and ended up at the doctor's office. The doctor told me something similar—that I was going to have to change the way I was living.

"But I didn't know what to change. Consequently, I suffered burnout within the next year and resigned. Later as the Pentecostals of Tri-Cities grew, I reflected on where I had gone wrong in my first pastorate. And one of those areas was not allowing the structure to change."

"You've mentioned several times about changes to the structure," Jon remarked. "Can you expand on that some?"

"Absolutely," said Pastor Chambers. "I was planning on it. Consider Acts 6. Some Greek-speaking Jews complained that certain widows were being overlooked in the daily distribution of food. You know the story, so I will skip retelling it. But here is something most people don't catch: Jesus chose twelve men to be His disciples. This inner core of leaders was responsible for overseeing the church. That was the original structure of the organization—twelve men who were chosen by Jesus. Jesus established that structure, and the structure remained.

"But after the Greek-speaking Jews complained, the twelve disciples considered the situation and recognized there was a leadership crisis. The growth of the organization—I'm using the word 'organization' as opposed to 'church' because I want to make a point here in a moment—was being threatened because of the structure. Thankfully, the twelve disciples changed the structure of the organization, and by doing so they addressed the leadership crisis. Are you still with me?"

"Yes. I'm following what you're saying," Jon assured. "This is all so very interesting."

Pastor Chambers continued, "Let me tell you why I'm using the word 'organization.' Every organization, whether it be government, for-profit, or nonprofit, undergoes what are called organizational life cycles. Multiple studies on this have been done around the world.

"The first cycle is the entrepreneurial stage. Success at this stage is on the shoulders of the leader. It is his vision, zeal, work ethic, commitment, know-how, and so on that make the organization thrive. If he lacks any of these things, the organization will struggle to grow.

"The challenge that all leaders of organizations face while the organization is in the entrepreneurial stage is that things eventually grow to where the leader can't do everything that needs to be done. Not that he doesn't have employees or help, but mostly it is all on him. If he isn't there on the scene, it will not work."

"That's exactly how I feel," Jon revealed. "It seems that almost everything falls on me. If I don't drive things forward, it doesn't happen. And the biggest problem I encounter with that is the lack of time. I simply don't have the time I need. If I were able to pastor full time, it would be different."

"Not necessarily," remarked Pastor Chambers. "While it is true you would have more time to do more stuff, it doesn't address the leadership crisis. In order to overcome the leadership crisis at the entrepreneurial stage, a leader must develop a team. That's what you need to be focusing on: the development of your team."

Jon said, "So if I'm hearing you correctly, the way to transition from the entrepreneurial stage to the next organizational life cycle stage is to get others involved . . . to develop a team."

"That is correct," Chambers affirmed. "The next stage in organizational life cycles is collectivity. In the collectivity stage, team members run with things that are handed off to them. Almost always during the collectivity stage, team members will attain job descriptions.

73

"These job descriptions are crucial to the success of the organization. Team members need to know what lane to run in, so to speak. Without job descriptions, leaders face a strong possibility of becoming frustrated with failure of others to _____ [you can fill in the blank with whatever]. In other words, things the leader is assuming others should do are not getting done. Ultimately, however, it is not the follower or employee's fault; it's the failure of the leader to take responsibility in spelling out his expectations.

"To recap, the leadership crisis in the entrepreneurial stage is that the leader is doing everything. He needs a team. And for members of the team to thrive, they need to know what the expectations are. It needs to be spelled out. They need to have ownership of their specific area.

"This is where Ben was struggling. This is also where I was struggling in my first pastorate. Ben and I both were trying to do most everything ourselves. And even when we started building teams, we never really empowered others to run with things.

"For example, during my first pastorate, when Easter came around, I took the lead in what the children's ministry needed to do. That is just one of many things I got involved with. And that's not the only ministry I took the lead in more times than not.

"Now here is the problem: Most of the time, the leaders were not taking the initiative in moving the ministry forward the way I thought they should. So I would get involved. But that was my fault, because I never took the time to develop job descriptions for the leaders. I just assumed they would know what to do. I even encouraged them to own the ministry, but I never helped establish the expectations in a job description. Hence, I never could get the monkey off my back.

"Ben was doing the same thing. He hired people. They would do what he told them to do, but he led every aspect of the business. And it was killing him. When it was just the food truck, he could handle it. But as things grew, the structure of his business had to grow too. The way Ben led had to change."

During Pastor Chambers's lengthy discourse, June and Shelly had been engrossed in their own conversation. When a server paused at their table to ask if they needed anything, June turned to Jon and said with amusement, "My husband loves talking about this stuff. I'm glad you're here so he has someone to share it with."

Jon said, "I'm glad I'm here too. I'm absorbing as much as I can." To which Shelly smiled and added, "Trust me, Jon loves this stuff. Pastor Chambers will get tired of talking before Jon stops asking for more."

Almost Done

Having taken his last bite of dessert, Pastor Chambers said, "Let me finish a couple of things before we go. After leaving the entrepreneurial stage and after fully engaging with the collectivity stage (everyone having job descriptions, knowing what to do, knowing what lane to run in, and so on) another leadership crisis forms.

"The leadership crisis in the collectivity stage is that team leaders know what to do, they own their ministry or department in a church, but when it comes to final decisions that need to be made, they go back to the leader.

"The crisis is that the leader is still involved in everything, as in giving detailed directions and approvals and so on within the organization. And remember, the organization has grown and there are so many things going on that the leader becomes spread too thin in giving all the approvals and directions needed. He becomes the bottleneck.

"And (this is very important) the leaders under him become stifled. Lacking the freedom to decide, leaders cannot grow; they're unable to fully function within the gifting that already exists. This causes lots of frustration for secondary leaders.

"Hence, the failure to allow structure to change is a growth inhibitor. If you're going to overcome growth inhibitors, one challenge will be in allowing the structure to change. And the struggle with that as a leader is that you have to be okay with not being involved in everything.

"And let me add that you have to be okay with people not doing things exactly the way you would do them. You have to be okay with allowing people to learn from their mistakes. You have to be okay with losing total control. This is a real challenge for most pastors. We don't like not having control. We need the control so we can put on a good presentation so people will be attracted to our churches and so that we can grow the church. But our job isn't necessarily about growing the church; it's about growing people."

Jon took a deep breath as he thought about how this different mindset could have such far-reaching effects. Focusing on growing the church ultimately stifles the growth of people, and the stifled growth of people ultimately stifles the growth of the church. *And it all starts with leadership*, thought Jon.

He blurted, "It's hard to admit, but unbeknownst to me, the issue in our situation has largely been me. But now I'm seeing it. Because I wanted to control things, I haven't allowed the church structure to change. When our church grew, my load of responsibilities increased. When I added team members, the same thing happened."

He paused and then continued as if he were receiving even more revelation, "Instead of empowering people, I've been delegating things to people. And why? Because of my fear of letting go of things, of not being in control. Wow, it's interesting how one's philosophies can have such a far-reaching impact on one's behaviors. And behaviors always result in one's destination. This means that if I don't like where things are, I'm going to have to change."

Pastor Chambers's smile seemed to reach from ear to ear, knowing Jon had just mentioned another growth inhibitor he planned to cover later. It was great to see that Pastor Jon was taking it all to heart and connecting the dots. "Well, it sounds like you've got it," said Pastor Chambers. "And that, my friend, is exciting. It's getting late, and tomorrow is a full day. Let's connect after service. You know what to do; just find your way back to my office whenever you want to, and we'll decide where to go eat. Maybe Greg Hyatt, our administrative pastor, and his wife can join us for lunch. We can have some additional discussion as to structure before you all head home."

After Service

The service had been as outstanding as on their first visit. Having carried so much of the load week after week, it was so refreshing to just show up and soak it all in. Of course, Jon and Shelly knew that would not be a good habit for anyone to acquire—being content to soak it all in. But for just one Sunday it was the perfect thing. Both of them admitted later that they needed it. Ultimately, they decided to take at least one Sunday a quarter to either go out of town or bring someone in to minister. The break from carrying the load would be rejuvenating.

Having gathered in the office after service, the Myerses enjoyed connecting with the church leaders they had met previously. After some time of greeting guests and connecting with some people, Pastor Chambers joined them.

It wasn't long before the plans for dinner were completed. Just as Pastor Chambers had hoped, the administrative pastor, Greg Hyatt, and his wife, Melissa, would be joining them. Everyone else had other plans. It couldn't have worked out better than it did.

After everyone ordered their food, Pastor Chambers jumped right in. "Pastor Greg," he remarked, "Pastor Jon and I have been talking about overcoming growth inhibitors. This weekend we focused on how a static structure can become a growth inhibitor and the importance of leaders allowing the structure to change. I would like for you to share with him your thoughts concerning the pushback some have with structure not being a spiritual thing."

"Sure," said Pastor Greg. "As you know, I serve as administrative pastor. I also preach and teach, but my strength lays within the details. I enjoy behind-the-scenes work, doing things that help the church function to its fullest capacity and accomplish its mission of equipping believers.

"We host various conferences and church-leader-ship seminars at the Pentecostals of Tri-Cities. Over the course of the past ten years, I would estimate that I have been the speaker for somewhere in the neighborhood of seventy-five to one hundred sessions, and that is just in our home church. It doesn't include the sessions I've taught elsewhere.

"Here's my point: The number-one pushback I've heard against structure is that it makes the church into an organization when it is in fact a spiritual organism. Many seem to think that if we have great church services, that will be the answer to growth, whether individually or corporately. But that isn't accurate. I'm sure you've heard of Evan Roberts and the Welsh Revival."

Jon acknowledged, "I've heard of the Welsh Revival, but I've never studied it."

Warming to the subject, Pastor Greg continued, "Here, then, are a few insights concerning that revival. One, it wasn't built around preaching as much as it was around singing and praying. Also, there was little to no structure at all. The people would sing and pray, and whoever felt like saying something could share whenever they felt led to do so.

"The revival had an amazing impact on the nation and beyond, including Azusa Street. In Wales, factories closed down at lunch as people flocked to churches for prayer. Rick Joyner tells the story in his book *The World Aflame: The Welsh Revival and Its Lessons for Our Time*.

"But as quickly as it came, the revival left. Joyner remarks that within just a few short years there was little to no sign that the revival had ever occurred. Interestingly—and this is the point according to Joyner—William Booth, founder of Salvation Army, visited the Welsh Revival. William Booth was a prominent evangelist during his time. We can see his evangelistic emphasis in the very name 'Salvation

Army.' Booth's desire was to use humanitarian efforts to lead people to salvation. Everything was about getting people saved.

"Now think about this," Pastor Jon said. "The Welsh Revival ended because it had no structure. In contrast, the mission of the Salvation Army looks nothing like it did when it started; it began, in so many words, as a church. But it isn't a church today. And according to Joyner, one reason is because it was too structured.

"One entity had no structure; the other was too focused on structure. Now what I've witnessed in most Pentecostal churches is a lack of structure. Personally, I believe balance is needed," Pastor Greg said.

"That makes sense," remarked Jon. "It reminds me of something I've heard here and there: Once our life is over, our ministry has ended. Hence, although our bodies aren't the most important thing, they are an important element of our ministries. We can't have ministry without our bodies."

"That's exactly right," Pastor Greg agreed. "It's a principle that applies to what I've been talking about. Structure matters. Balance matters." He went on to say, "The other pushback I hear is that structure is big-church stuff; it isn't for small-size churches. But that's not true. The reason many pastors are so overwhelmed doing everything is because of a lack of structure. Implementing structure, even if it's only job descriptions for various ministry leaders, would take some work on the front end, but it would free pastors up so they could focus solely on the things they alone can do."

The men talked for some time concerning the ins and outs of structure. Pastor Chambers remarked that Pastor Greg and the Pentecostals of Tri-Cities' ministerial team would do their best to help in establishing needed structure at Greater Life Church.

Jon thanked them profusely and added that he would take them up on their offer. He was determined to overcome the third growth inhibitor. He was going to do his best, along with the help of the Tri-Cities pastors, to work on the structure of Greater Life Church.

REASON
NUMBER FOUR

COMMUNICATE A COMPELLING PURPOSE

J on was frustrated, and he couldn't wait to talk with Pastor Chambers about it. Originally they had scheduled another meeting on the river since now both men loved fly-fishing. Thunderstorms, however, had blanketed the area, so that was out.

Admittedly, Jon was disappointed he wouldn't be able to spend the day on the river learning more about fly-fishing, but his frustration stemmed from his efforts to make changes to the structure of Greater Life Church. He had sought to apply what he'd been learning from his meetings with Pastor Chambers. He had invited others to the table and had paid close attention to the various personality types, adjusting his approach accordingly.

Yet, surprisingly to Jon, there had been resistance. One leader had remarked that job descriptions as well as the additional forms Jon wanted the leaders to fill out (event-request dates, announcement forms, budget requests, and so on) all seemed too businesslike, and he didn't know what to do about it.

Later after the team meeting was over, a leader informed him that one of the team members had said, "What works at a big church won't work here." Clearly the remark was meant as a pushback against Jon bringing to the church things he had learned at the Pentecostals of Tri-Cities.

Jon's immediate thought was, *I shouldn't have invited them to the table if that's the way it's going to be. After all, I'm the pastor.* But that thought was quickly replaced with another: *We can't keep doing the things we've been doing and get to where we need to go.*

But as for what to do, he was uncertain.

The Meeting

The men had decided to meet at Pastor Chambers's office. This allowed both men to spend some time in the morning focusing on their messages for Sunday.

Upon arriving at the church, Jon noticed some ladies were leaving and rightfully assumed they had been at early-morning prayer. He couldn't help but wish for the day when the same thing was occurring at Greater Life Church: people engaged in an array of activities.

While making his way to the pastor's office, he noticed a team of people assembled in the conference room. He thought it might have had something to do with the evangelism team as he recognized a few of its members in the meeting.

Rounding the corner, he arrived at the senior pastor's office. He knocked on the door and heard Pastor Chambers call out, "Come in." Jon opened the door and noticed that Pastor Chambers was busily grabbing books from the stack on his desk and placing them on a bookshelf.

"Good morning! Great to see you," said Pastor Chambers heartily. "Parden me, I'm just about done."

"I'm glad to see you," said Jon. "Have you bought some new books?"

Chuckling, Pastor Chambers remarked, "Every week. I love to read. These are some books I've been reading at home. I'm running out of space on my bookshelves there and thought I would bring them to the office."

After exchanging a few more pleasantries, the two were comfortably settled in and ready for some meaningful conversation.

"How are things going?" Pastor Chambers inquired. The way he said it one could easily see he was asking Jon to be transparent and forthcoming. And Jon was more than ready to share his frustration. He told Pastor Chambers all that had happened—how he had called a meeting with some leaders to work on putting some structure into place. He hadn't told everybody what to do; instead, he had invited others to the table.

Jon described how he had done his best to allow others to have a voice, that he had shared the overall big picture but had welcomed, even asked, for everyone's input into shaping the structure and designing what it would look like in reality.

Then he described some statements that had been made, the resistance he had felt from a couple people who had been invited to the table. Jon added that he'd done his best to look at the resistance in light of the differences in personalities and opined that those differences in personalities didn't give anyone the right to be critical of the changes that needed to take place. Last, Jon remarked that he wondered if the people who had spoken against some of the changes were against him as pastor.

During this unloading, Pastor Chambers's facial expression conveyed he was listening intently.

As Jon finished sharing his frustrations, Pastor Chambers smiled and said, "Well, that doesn't sound too unusual."

Jon thought, *What?! That doesn't sound too unusual?* He didn't say it aloud, but Pastor Chambers must have read his mind because he asked, "What did you expect, Pastor Jon?"

"I'm not sure," Jon admitted. "I guess I thought learning about how to overcome growth inhibitors was supposed to help me, not hurt me." He didn't add that on the drive over he had thought a few times about the meeting and wondered if his learning the growth inhibitors was a waste of his time.

Resistance

Jon opened up and shared a little more than he had planned on. "Pastor Chambers, I appreciate the time you've taken for me. And I've certainly been affected by it all. But I have a question I can't get out of my mind. I've heard you talk about overcoming various growth inhibitors by inviting others to the table, celebrating differences, and embracing an ever-growing structure.

"What I haven't heard you talk about in overcoming growth inhibitors is prayer and fasting and preaching and teaching doctrine—things like that. Do you think the resistance I encountered would be best addressed by simply having a move of God? Seems to me if people would just experience a revival in their heart, everything else would just fall into place."

Pastor Chambers asked kindly, "Do you think we at Tri-Cities don't pray and fast and preach sound doctrine?"

"Oh, I'm sure you do," Jon said hastily. "That's not what I meant. I'm just saying that when I think of growth inhibitors, I think of spiritual battles, carnality, and so on. You have yet to deal with anything of that nature. You've even suggested that the principles in overcoming the growth inhibitors apply to any type of organization. Don't misunderstand me; everything we've discussed has been good.

"But it just seems to me that as a church if we were to pray more, fast more, engage in heartfelt worship, sacrifice more, be more committed, and so on, that we wouldn't have to be so concerned about structure and differences in personalities and inviting others to the table. Wouldn't those things take care of themselves if we would just be spiritual people?"

Without waiting for a reply, Jon continued, "Please don't misunderstand me, Pastor Chambers. I respect you highly; I am just sharing my feelings about it all. Just trying to be transparent."

Pastor Chambers assured, "You're okay. Don't worry about it. I want to hear what you're feeling. Now let's think about it. As we mentioned in one of our previous conversations, the early church in Acts 6 encountered resistance from some Greek-speaking Jews regarding the widows. How did the apostles respond?

Did they rebuke these people? Did they call the church to prayer? Did they preach on unity?

"No. They recognized the heart of the matter. The issue was structure related, along with some preexisting societal prejudice. They rightfully addressed the issue by changing the structure and allowing the church to choose seven men to oversee the distribution of goods. And it appears, based on the names of those chosen men, these men were Greek-speaking Jews, thus addressing the preexisting societal prejudice."

Pastor Chambers then asked, "What happened with the church after this structural change? It experienced great growth, and many priests even became believers. The Bible doesn't mention a prayer meeting. It doesn't mention that the apostles reprimanded those who were complaining. They didn't preach any sermons addressing gossip or the need for unity. Does that mean the church wasn't praying or that the apostles were not preaching?"

Before Jon could answer, Pastor Chambers said, "Here's the question I really want you to consider: What would you have done if you had been in the apostles' shoes? How would you have handled the situation?"

The question at first stumped Jon. But after thinking about it a moment, he realized he needed to analyze his feelings based on the example Pastor Chambers had cited. Finally, he admitted, "I doubt I would have handled it like the apostles did. But that still doesn't negate the importance of prayer and fasting and sound doctrine."

"Of course not," replied Pastor Chambers. "Let me ask you another question. I'm sure you are a praying man, but if you are human like me, you probably experience times in which you're not as given to spiritual disciplines as you should be. Is that correct?"

"That is correct," Jon affirmed.

"And I'm assuming you take part in fasting and other spiritual disciplines, but sometimes it's easier than other times. And sometimes you probably end up lacking. Is that correct?" he asked.

"Yes," said Jon. "I hate to admit it, but sometimes I'm not as disciplined as I probably should be."

"Okay," said Pastor Chambers with a smile. "Stay with me a minute. I'm going somewhere with all of this."

Jon said, "That sounded just like a preacher." Both men laughed.

Pastor Chamber asked, "Have you ever heard of the difference between lag measures and lead measures?"

"I don't think so."

"Then let me explain. Lag measures focus on measuring the past; lead measures measure things that end up leading you to where you want to go. For example, suppose you want to lose weight."

"Wait a minute," Jon interjected, laughing. "Are you saying I'm fat?"

"Oh no," remarked Pastor Chambers with a chuckle. "This is just an illustration. But . . ." Both men shared a laugh.

Continuing, Pastor Chamber said, "If you want to lose weight, weighing yourself on a scale will only reveal what has happened in the past—the impact of the ice cream you ate, the lack of exercise, and so on. But what if you were to measure calories for your meals? Or monitor your portions? Or establish a certain amount of exercise each day? Such things are called lead measures. They lead you where you want to go. Does that make sense?"

"It sure does," said Jon.

"Good. Now consider this: Let's go back to what we were talking about a few minutes ago. If you were in one of those lull moments in time, let's say with your prayer time, and you received a call to speak at a ministers' conference, do you think you would be led to spend some time in prayer?"

"Absolutely," replied Jon. "But it shouldn't be that way," he added.

"That is true," said Pastor Chambers. "Again, this is only an illustration. I'm just trying to make a point."

"I'm a little confused," said Jon. "We started off talking about the resistance I encountered when I tried to install some structure. And now we're talking about my prayer life. I'm not sure I'm connecting all the dots." He paused and then asked, "Are you suggesting that I'm the problem? That my occasional lull in prayer causes the resistance I encountered?"

Pastor Chambers laughed. "Not in the slightest. I am saying, however, that it's common for people to be motivated to do the right things, such as pray, when they are engaged in something that leads them to pray."

"Oh," said Jon as the lightbulb of understanding flashed. "I think I'm getting it."

"Think about this," continued Pastor Chambers. "Do you recall one of our earlier conversations when we said that at the Pentecostals of Tri-Cities we're not interested in getting caught up in a numbers game? Instead, we use numbers to help us know where we might need to place some emphasis."

"Yes. I do remember that," answered Jon.

"I think it was the first time you met Bob Cain, our growth pastor."

"Oh yes. I definitely remember him saying that."

"Well, here's a little more insight. Sunday attendance is a lag measure. It reveals the past. What do you think might be a lead measure?"

"Well, if I recall that conversation correctly, coupled with some of what you've been teaching me, a lead measure would be to count the number of people engaged in growth classes. Or the number of Bible studies being taught. Or the . . ."

Pastor Chambers interrupted. "That's it!" he said enthusiastically. "Those are the type of things that lead people to growth. Sorry for the interruption, but you've got it! Now let me ask you this: What percentage of churches focus on lead measures? On measuring things that lead to where they want to go?"

Jon had to admit that most churches he'd been associated with did not focus on lead measures.

"Think about this too," said Pastor Chambers. "Most sermons on prayer focus on how we ought to pray and that we aren't praying like we should. Do you think such messages lead us to pray? To a certain extent, I guess you could say they do in that they make people feel guilty. But how long does that last? A day or two? Maybe a week or so?"

Continuing, he said, "What if, instead, we taught people how to teach Bible studies? Not that they *ought* to teach Bible studies but *how* to teach Bible studies. What if we showed them how to make disciples? What if we were to structure how we 'do' church and made it more conducive for people to make disciples? To actually take time to invite people to journey life with them by discipling them? Do you think a person engaged in teaching Bible studies would be more apt to pray than someone who simply sits on a church pew? What about the couple discipling others? Do you think they would be more apt to walk close to the Lord and have a God-pleasing marriage than the couple who just shows up to church on Sunday morning only? Are you getting the point?" asked Pastor Chambers.

Jon nodded, beginning to envision the possibilities.

"Think about it," said Pastor Chamber, returning to the original issue. "You received some negative feedback from a few you invited to the table. It bothers you, doesn't it?"

Jon nodded in agreement and added, "Yes, somewhat."

"Do you think that if you hadn't invited them to the table they never would have thought that or said it behind closed doors?"

Jon didn't like where the senior pastor was going, but he acknowledged to himself that Pastor Chambers likely was right.

"Do you think the invitation to the table created the resistance?" Pastor Chambers continued. "Or do you think the resistance still would have been there, but you would have been oblivious to it?"

Jon knew Pastor Chambers was right. Those who expressed resistance likely would have felt the same way regardless, and he likely wouldn't have known about it.

"Furthermore," said Pastor Chambers, "you now have an advantage that you didn't have before. Now that the resistance is out in the open, you can deal with it rightly, whereas before you would've had to move forward without support from key members without knowing why.

"So here's the ultimate question: Would you rather know what people are thinking so you can address their concerns, or would you rather be oblivious to it all?"

"That's a hard one," said Jon. "I see the value in knowing. Yet it's frustrating too. And their negative expressions could have swayed the rest of the group in the wrong direction."

"First," replied Pastor Chambers, "I seriously doubt their comments would have sidetracked everyone else in the wrong direction. Instead, I would think that others in the group probably felt even stronger about the need for what you were advocating. Am I right?"

Jon admitted he probably was right. "Several of the members approached me afterward, saying the changes were needed in order to get to where we wanted to go. One person even added that they had been hoping we would change our structure because they had seen our current lack of it as a hinderance for quite some time."

"I know the entire matter is frustrating," said Pastor Chambers. "But you can't allow a few bumps in the road to deter you from where you're headed."

Focusing on Purpose

Pastor Chambers suggested, "I've got an idea. Let's take a drive out to Ben's Place. With the rain, there won't be a large crowd. We can find a quiet place to sit. His lunch menu is outstanding, as you well know."

"I think that's a great idea," said Jon.

On the way to Ben's Place, the conversation picked back up with an ever-so-slight twist in the subject.

Pastor Chamber began, "Let's talk a little about purpose. This is something I had planned on sharing with you, and it goes hand in hand with what we've been discussing this morning. Defining the purpose of something—whether it's an organization, church, nonprofit, team, or even an initiative—is an essential element in achieving success. As leaders, one of the most important roles we fulfill is making sure those who follow know the purpose.

"The purpose not only has to be clear, but it must be compelling. If the purpose is clear and compelling, the members of—let's just focus on a team—will come together. If the purpose isn't compelling or clearly understood, members of a team will not come together. The value of a team isn't the sum of the individuals' efforts; the value of a team is the synergy generated by all the team members working together. Do you get what I mean?"

"Yes," replied Jon. "That reminds me of a story I once read about the power of a Belgian draft horse. One Belgian can pull eight thousand pounds. But they found that if they put two Belgians in the harness, even if those horses were strangers to each other, together they could pull between twenty thousand and twenty-four thousand pounds."

"That's fantastic!" Pastor Chambers exclaimed. "I was aware of the gist of that story, but I didn't know the details. The same is true for teams," he continued. "If the purpose is unclear or it isn't compelling, the members of a team will not come together. Then their efforts will be the sum of the individual members of the team, and the members most likely won't be giving it their best effort.

"But when the purpose is clear and compelling, it's the glue that binds together a group of individuals. It's what causes members of a team to come together. When they come together, it creates synergy. Great things can be accomplished when members of a team come together.

"Unfortunately, even within churches, members are all doing their own thing. This often results in duplicated work, pursuit of self-interest, and so on. It isn't the best that we could offer, not by any means."

Past Chambers reflected, "I believe most people want to achieve success. No one wants to be a loser. The vast majority of people want to be part of something larger and more important than themselves. Most people are searching for significance. They want their life to matter. For instance, I read the other day that 83 percent of workers said it was 'very important' to them that their lives were meaningful; and another 15 percent said it was 'fairly important.' Together, that is 98 percent of people who say it's important that their lives are meaningful.

"That is astonishing to me. Purpose matters, and it matters a great deal. No wonder one of the foremost things a new team should do is make sure the purpose is clear and compelling. If it is, the synergy or power of a group is amazing to contemplate. There's no telling what a group can accomplish."

Jon remarked, "That reminds me of the building of the Tower of Babel. Didn't God say something to the effect that because the people were one, nothing they set out to do would be impossible for them?"

"Exactly," replied Pastor Chambers. "That is the power of purpose. The only problem with the building of the Tower of Babel was that it was the wrong purpose." Pastor Chambers paused and then said, "You know, I've never thought of it before, but that makes a good point, Pastor Jon. Making sure the purpose is clearly understood is so important. If it isn't, people may unite around a wrong purpose instead of the right one."

Jon nodded in agreement. "They would arrive at the wrong destination if the purpose wasn't clear."

Pastor Chambers said, "So, let's put it all together. You have to know that the destination matters, that the cause is worthy of the effort. And you have to translate that to the team.

Now let me ask you this question: What is the purpose of the structure you are trying to implement? Can you articulate it? Is it worthy of the hassle that comes with change? Is it compelling? And perhaps most important, I believe you understand the purpose and believe it's compelling, but does your team understand it? Or do they just think you want to be like the Pentecostals of Tri-Cities?"

Once again, Jon was stumped. Then it suddenly became clear where he had gone wrong; he had failed to share with the team a worthy and compelling purpose for implementing the changes to the structure.

After a moment of silence, Jon admitted as much. "I can see where I went wrong. I failed to take the time to articulate the purpose. How could I have missed that?"

Pastor Chambers smiled and said, "Don't be too hard on yourself. It's a common thing. Many leaders just assume that everyone gets it, but few take the time to make sure that team members are aligned with the purpose."

Continuing, Pastor Chambers remarked, "This is also why you often see silo ministries within a church. Everyone is doing their own thing. It isn't that there's a lack of purpose; the problem is there is no one central, worthy purpose for everyone to rally around. So they end up with an abundance of less-than-ideal purposes."

Jon was taken aback by all he had just heard. If someone had asked him yesterday, "Do your team members understand the purpose?" he would have said yes. But now he understood his assumption was incorrect. The reason he had encountered resistance is that the team was unaware of the worthy and compelling purpose for the needed changes to the structure.

Pulling into the parking lot at Ben's Place, Pastor Chambers remarked, "One last thing about purpose—for now that is. Not just any lofty-sounding purpose will work. Unless a purpose is backed with substance, as in research or truth, rarely will it ever generate excitement. A purpose has to be real, it has to be tangible, and it has to be compelling if people are going to engage in it."

Ben's Place

It was just as Pastor Chambers assumed. Because of the weather, Ben's Place wasn't as busy as usual. In just a short time they were settled at a table in a quiet place with a great view of the outdoors. In spite of the rain, the scene had a certain beauty.

After ordering their meal, Pastor Chambers said, "Recently I was reading a book in which the author told an intriguing story. He said that shortly after a new hospital administrator assumed her position at the hospital, she discovered that the custodial staff had some major issues. Morale was low, turnover was high, and staff performance was definitely lacking."

He looked at Jon. "What would you do if you were in that position? Figure out whom to fire?"

Jon mused, "I'm not sure what I would do. But I know if I were to fire people and something else was at the root of the situation, and I didn't address that root, then firing people would lower the morale even further. So I reckon I would try to uncover the root cause of the low morale."

"Great answer," said Pastor Chambers. "That's basically what the administrator did. She said that things changed for the positive when she officially recognized the real purpose of the custodians' jobs—they were key members of the hospital's 'Infection Control Team.'"

"I guess that means their purpose was bigger than just keeping the floors clean," remarked Jon.

"Yes. They played an essential role in controlling the spread of infection throughout the hospital. In your situation, Pastor Jon, I surmise you encountered resistance from some who were struggling in understanding the purpose for structure or the need for changes to be made to that structure. Again, the purpose has to be a worthy and compelling one."

Jon thought, *I can use this at work! Here I am in HR, and we're struggling with various things that, at the root, have a lack of alignment with purpose. And at church . . . this makes so much sense!*

Finally, Jon spoke, "I guess I assumed that everyone understood the purpose. But I was wrong. I failed to convey the importance of what we were doing in making changes to the structure. In fact, I've failed multiple times, as I've been reflecting back to various situations in conveying the purpose. Right now, I'd say that's the biggest reason people don't follow through with commitment: they don't see the value in what they have committed to do."

As the food arrived, Pastor Chambers made his final points concerning purpose, "Although the purpose needs to be highly compelling, it also must be made tangible. It has to be able to be converted into concrete goals and plans. One might say it like this: Team members not only need to know that what they're doing is important, which is the purpose, they have to know where they're headed, which is the goal and the plan.

"I admit this isn't always easy. And it isn't a onetime event in which you identify and talk about purpose. You have to constantly orbit around the purpose; it has to be the center. You yourself can't be the center because you're not the purpose. You can be near the center, but you can't *be* the center. We'll talk more about all of that at a later time.

"Just know this: if you can get people aligned with the purpose and orbiting around the purpose, just about everything else will come into the right position. This includes things like roles and responsibilities, mutual values and expectations, and so on. These things shape the culture of a church. They also will provide the means for ongoing performance assessment."

Jon, busily taking notes, thought to himself, *It's a good thing I brought my notebook with me into the restaurant. Seems like lots of good things take place while seated at a table.* He smiled.

As he had done a few times previously, Pastor Chambers said, "While you're taking notes, put this down. It's something I want you to consider occasionally as you reflect on your team. Ask yourself if your team is a cohesive team that is functioning at the highest level possible. If it isn't, consider this first: Is the purpose your team is pursuing a worthy and compelling purpose? For instance, are you helping people save lives from infection, or do you just have them scrubbing floors?"

Jon looked up from his notes. "You've just helped me more than you know, Pastor Chambers. This is powerful stuff. In many ways defining purpose seems so small that it's easy to overlook—one of those things we assume people get but they don't." He then added, "But perhaps most important is that it is causing me to reevaluate some things. Like why are we doing some of the things we're doing? Is it really a worthy and compelling purpose, or are we just busying doing stuff that, while it may be okay, isn't really that important?"

He finished, "I can't wait to talk with Shelly about all of this."

Ben's Place, Again

Just about the time the Jon finished his remarks, Pastor Chambers looked up to see Ben walk into the dining room. He waved to get his friend's attention, and Ben hurried over to greet them.

Pastor Chambers said, "Ben, I want you to meet a new fly-fishing fanatic. This is a pastor friend of mine named Jon."

"So you're a fly-fishing fanatic like the two of us," said Ben.

"Not exactly," replied Jon, laughing. "But I want to be." Pastor Chambers and Ben shared the laugh.

Pastor Chambers invited, "Ben, do you have time to sit down and chat a little?"

"Absolutely," said Ben. "I wish I didn't have time, though. I was planning on spending at least half of the day on the river. But this rain ruined my plans."

"We wanted to fish too," said Pastor Chambers. "In fact, I had thought about calling you to see if you wanted to join us."

Jon said, "Next time we definitely have to make that happen. I've heard you're quite the fisherman."

Ben said, "I thought I was, until I met our pastor friend here. Then I knew for certain that I was."

Everyone laughed. Jon could easily tell that Pastor Chambers and Ben enjoyed each other's company. He said, "I don't know if it's appropriate for me to say this, Ben, but I heard a little about your story, about going from a food truck to this really great place. And Mary's Place too. That's so cool."

"Have you been to Mary's Place?" Ben inquired.

"I sure have," said Jon. "I took my wife there too. We loved it. We will definitely go back."

"Ben," said Pastor Chambers, "Can you share some of the backstory concerning the remodel and the expansion of the kitchen, especially when you hired a head cook to take over the operations?"

"Oh, *that* story," said Ben, chuckling. "It's a long story, so I'll just hit the highlights and then we can talk some more about fly-fishing. Well, here goes. Although I'd never done anything like it before, I hired a man named Jim as head chef. Jim had been trained at culinary school, but his knowledge didn't intimidate me, even though I was self-taught. But I figured with all of his schooling, he would want things done differently than the way I did them. And boy was I ever right!

"One night, practically the entire crew walked out on me, and it was my fault. Jim was a great guy—now owns his own place over on the far side of the city. I helped him get it started." Ben added with a touch of humor, "I even helped him name his restaurant: Jim's Place."

Jon laughed and said, "I could have guessed that."

Ben continued, "Anyway, that night (the night practically everyone walked out) I showed up at a busy time. The pace was hectic as the kitchen staff tried to keep up with orders. Overall, though, I later determined they were doing an okay job, and they didn't need my involvement. But at the moment, I thought I needed to get involved. So, I did.

"I started ordering people around. Of course, Jim quickly became frustrated, and the kitchen staff got agitated. Jim was telling them one thing, and then I would tell them something different. After several hours of this and many messed-up orders, Jim came to me and demanded that I get out of his kitchen. Needless to say, I didn't like that one bit and told him so. Of course, the confrontation escalated from there, and both of us ended up yelling nose to nose."

Caught up in the story, Jon asked, "What happened next?"

"Well," Ben hedged, "I guess I'll let Pastor Chambers tell that part."

Jon quickly glanced at Pastor Chambers, who laughed and said, "June and I were eating here that night, and our table was near the kitchen door. I heard the yelling, and before I knew it, I was standing inside the kitchen."

"Whew, was he ever a godsend!" Ben exclaimed as he once again took up the narrative. "Pastor Chambers looked at us and said, 'Guys, what are you doing?' Jim and I just glared at him. Then he said, 'You two have a business to run and a restaurant full of people. They don't care who's right or who's wrong. They just want some wonderful food in an incredible atmosphere. But you both are ruining it.' Then he turned and walked out."

Ben continued, "That was the night things started turning around. I learned the value of empowering someone as opposed to just delegating things. Our staff learned that although I was the owner, there were others who knew what to do and they could follow them and everything would be okay, even if it was different from how I would do things.

"Most of all, the lesson I learned that night was that nothing is more important than the main purpose. If you forget about the purpose, you'll get sidetracked with other things and think they are the most important. But they aren't. I can attest to that. Purpose is the most important thing."

Ben finished by saying, "And Jim . . . he's become one of my best friends. I learned a lot from him. And I taught him a few things too." Ben grinned.

Pastor Chambers said, "I almost didn't ask Ben to tell the story; I didn't want to highlight my involvement in it. But it is an amazing story about purpose. Ben overcame a growth inhibitor by leading his team to orbit around a worthwhile and compelling purpose."

Jon said, "Thank you both for sharing the story. It was awesome. But Pastor Chambers, I can't believe you just walked right into the kitchen! Then again—I guess I can. After all, you're a Dominant Driver." The men chuckled.

Ben said, "That's enough of all of that for now. Let's talk about fly-fishing!" And that's exactly what they did, including putting together plans for a fly-fishing trip in the fall.

Back at the hotel later that evening, Jon thought about the focus of the conversation that day—a worthy and compelling purpose. He could hardly wait to meet with his leadership team. There was a worthy purpose for it.

REASON
NUMBER FIVE

FOCUS ON VALUES
OVER PERFORMANCE

It had been nearly six weeks since Jon's last visit with Pastor Chambers. Much had occurred during that time period. First, his family had taken a vacation. Second, shortly after returning from their trip, the division within the company Jon worked for started working on a big initiative that would keep him busier than normal for the next few months.

Third, Jon was looking forward to the day when he could be full-time at the church. He was hoping it wouldn't be much longer, maybe a year or two. In the meantime, however, he was committed to the journey no matter what it took.

Last, there had been several special events and services at Greater Life Church. Thankfully, the team had stepped up to shoulder much of the weight. The follow-up meeting with the team regarding improvements to the structure had been a success. Jon was confident everyone now understood the purpose for the changes.

While there was still much more work to be done, the implementation of simple job descriptions accompanied by the list of responsibilities and expectations had helped team members feel empowered. It couldn't have come at a better time.

Pastor Chambers had texted often, asking how things were going. Jon had called him once to fill him in on how the meeting with the team had gone.

Due to their busy schedules, the men decided to meet halfway. They would start out at a coffeehouse. Later, before heading home, they would eat at Shelly's favorite steakhouse, the one where she and Jon were supposed to have eaten the night he had counseled the couple with marital problems. Shelly and the children already had plans to spend the day with her parents, and she playfully teased Jon about not getting to go once again.

The Coffeehouse

Jon arrived early. He had planned it that way since he hadn't finished studying for Sunday. After ordering his coffee, he settled at a table, took out his laptop, and delved into what he'd been working on. By the time Pastor Chambers walked in, Jon was ready for a second cup of coffee.

"Did I get the time wrong?" asked Pastor Chambers. "It looks like you've been here awhile."

"No," said Jon. "You're right on time. I came a little earlier to finish some of my studying for tomorrow's message. I also wanted to make sure we had a table. You never know on a Saturday how crowded it might be. As it is, I think we are meeting late enough that we have missed most of the morning rush."

After a few more pleasantries, they settled in for a conversation concerning how overcoming growth inhibitors can lead to a thriving church. Pastor Chambers had said previously that while there are many growth inhibitors, he was going to focus on just five of them—the five that were, according to his perspective, the most common for churches. He had also emphasized that each one of the growth inhibitors could be overcome. Jon was looking forward to the discussion; he was eager to learn more.

The Lesson

Pastor Chambers dove into a meaningful conversation: "Many years ago during my first pastorate, I counseled a couple who were in the throes of marital difficulties. In fact, I wasn't sure they would stay together.

"Here is the context of their story: The husband had committed adultery. At the time I entered the picture, the couple had been separated for several months. I didn't know either one of them, but I agreed to get involved because the pastor of one of the spouses was a close friend of mine. That pastor had already spoken with the pastor of the other spouse, and the two of them had decided a totally unbiased party—me—would be the best person to help them.

"Everything the husband said during our first meeting was the best I could have hoped for. He was apologetic and expressed great remorse for what he had done. He said he had asked for forgiveness multiple times and that he wanted their marriage to work. However, he also added that he wasn't sure what else he could do. Things seemed stuck and there had been no improvement.

"I couldn't get the wife to talk much at all. In fact, when they walked into the office, I was expecting them to sit on the same couch. But that didn't happen. He sat down on one end of the couch. She found a chair as far away from him as she could.

"Thinking about it later, it made sense, but it certainly wasn't what I was expecting. I was expecting both of the spouses to come to the counseling session with at least some measure of interest in seeing if they could work things out. Based on her body language, though, I concluded she was only there because her pastor had asked her to go.

"I did my best to ask open-ended questions . . . questions designed to get her talking. But she would give me the shortest answer possible without looking me in the eye. After our first session, I had little hope for their marriage. I saw no sign of her giving him another chance. Things were at an impasse.

"About thirty to forty minutes into our next session, I started praying. I still made no headway in getting her to open up, and he was merely repeating what he'd said the week before. I remember thinking that I should have told my pastoral friend I couldn't be of any help. Instead of meeting with me, the couple should be meeting with a marriage counselor. I was fairly certain they had come to the wrong guy for help, and I was absolutely certain this would be my last counseling session with the couple.

"But inspiration suddenly came to me; I thought of an illustration I'd never used before. It was truly a God moment. Rising from my chair, I positioned myself behind it. I then asked the couple, 'Who is going to sit in this chair?' They looked at me as if to say, 'Probably you. You're the one who's been sitting in it.'" Pastor Chambers grinned and Jon laughed.

The senior pastor continued, "I told them, 'Let's say there's only one chair in the room. Who's going to sit in it? Will it be you, or you?' I pointed at each spouse. I then said, pointing at the husband, 'This is what I see.

I see you sitting in this chair, and you're saying you've done everything you know to do. You have repented. You have asked for forgiveness. There's nothing more you can do. So you're going to sit in the chair and expect your wife to orbit around you.' And I started walking around the chair."

Jon was leaning forward, listening intently.

Pastor Chambers continued, "I then pointed at the wife and said, 'I see you sitting in the chair. You're saying you forgave him a long time ago, but you don't trust him. Therefore, you're going to sit in this chair, and you want him to orbit around you.' So my question to you both is, 'Who's going to sit in this chair?'

"The two of them just sat there in complete silence. I then asked the husband if he loved God. He replied that he did. So I asked him again, 'Do you *really* love God?' and he said yes. Then I asked him, 'Do you love God enough that if you were to get back together again with your wife and she made your life miserable for the next twenty years, would you still live for Him?' With tears in his eyes, he said, 'Yes. I love God that much.'

"I responded, 'I believe you.' And I really did.

"Looking at the wife, I asked, 'Do you love God?' She said yes. I then asked her again, 'Do you *really* love God?' and again she replied yes. So I said, 'Let's suppose you decide to reconcile as a couple and only two years later he has another affair. Will you still love God? Will you still live for Him despite what has happened?' Looking up at me, she said, 'Yes, I love God that much.'"

Pastor Chamber declared, "I will never forget the moment. I was still standing behind my chair, and upon hearing how much she loved God, I clapped my hands and said, 'Congratulations! You all are going to have a great marriage!' They looked at me like I'd lost my mind.

"Mind you, the husband was still sitting on his end of the couch and the wife was still sitting in a chair as far away from him as she could get. I explained, 'You both just told me who is going to sit on the chair—neither one of you. The Lord is going to sit in this chair, and together you're going to orbit around Him.'

"Then looking at the husband I said, 'Because you love the Lord and are going to allow Him to sit in the chair, you're going to give your wife every password to every piece of technology you own. When she calls you on the phone to check on what you're doing, you're going to answer with kindness. You're going to reassure her by telling her where you are and who you're with. Even if she calls you multiple times a day, you're going to answer with kindness every time. Because you're the one who broke trust, it's going to be your burden to restore it. And you are going to do these things because the Lord is the One sitting in the chair.'

"Turning to the wife, I said, 'Because you love the Lord, you're going to forgive and choose not to recall what has happened. I'm not saying you will ever forget it; you will always know what he did. But you'll choose to never bring it back up and use it for vindictive purposes. You're going to do this because you love the Lord, and He is the One sitting on the chair. You will orbit around Him.'"

Jon asked eagerly, "So how did things work out?"

"Just as I said," replied Pastor Chambers. "I told them they were going to have a wonderful marriage, and they did. What did you expect?" he said, laughing.

Jon laughed too.

Pastor Chambers said, "That was years ago. From time to time, I receive a message from them thanking me for all I did. To be honest, I don't feel I had much to do with it. It was a God thing. I must say, however, that I benefited as much, if not more, from the counseling session than the couple I counseled. I didn't realize at the moment how vital it would be in my own life. But over the next few years, the Lord used the chair illustration to teach me a central principle about leadership. I've applied the principle in multiple ways and have shared it with many leaders.

"The principle is simple. What you choose to orbit around matters. As a leader, it's much better to lead others to orbit around the common purpose and core values than it is to orbit around oneself."

Pastor Jon asked, "Help me understand something so I can make sure I'm getting it. The last time we met, we talked about purpose and how if you don't have a worthy and compelling purpose, people will get sidetracked. Alignment comes through understanding a worthy and compelling purpose. But now you're saying that right alongside the importance of purpose is the importance in orbiting around core values. Can you expand on what you mean by core values?"

Before Pastor Chambers could respond, Jon continued, "Let me say, really quick, before you answer . . . I'm aware of the concept of core values. Most businesses have a set of values, often posted on a sign near the door. We have a set of values at my job. They're posted on the wall right behind the receptionist's desk when you enter the offices. Are you suggesting that we need a sign in the church lobby that states our values?"

"Not necessarily," said Pastor Chambers, "although, a sign somewhere stating your values isn't a bad idea.

But ultimately, I'm not into creating nice-sounding value statements. I'm much more interested in making sure our team understands our core values and that we are aligned with them.

"Far too many businesses have a value statement, or stated values, but are not living out what they claim to adhere to. Consider the Enron Corporation. I'm sure you've heard of them. The company was named 'America's Most Innovative Company' by *Fortune* magazine for six consecutive years from 1996–2001. Its stated values were *integrity, communication, respect, and excellence*. These values were painted on the wall and displayed in their annual report. Nothing wrong with any of that.

"The problem was, however, that it was all a sham. The leaders of the company professed values they were not abiding by. Although the revenues and profits they touted looked good, they weren't real. They were purposefully misleading everyone.

"In December 2001, Enron filed for bankruptcy. It was the largest bankruptcy in American corporate history. The scandal also destroyed Arthur Anderson, their auditor, which at the time was one of the world's top five accounting firms and had been in business nearly a hundred years.

"Pastor Jon, am I correct that you're asking about the correlation of purpose and core values?"

"Yes," replied Jon.

"Well," said Pastor Chambers, "I think Enron offers the perfect example. Without alignment with core values, an organization could attempt to achieve a good purpose the wrong way. Purpose is the *why* we do what we do; values tell us *how* we are to do it."

"Say that again," Jon requested.

As Pastor Chambers repeated it, Jon wrote in his notebook, "Purpose is about the *why*; values are about the *how*."

"So let me see if I'm getting this correctly," remarked Jon. "The couple you counseled . . . the *why* would be to give God glory, whereas the *how* would be in the various values that support the why. Does that make sense?"

"Absolutely," Pastor Chambers affirmed. "Now let's apply that within the context of a church. At the Pentecostals of Tri-Cities, our *why* (our purpose) is to make disciples, followers of Jesus Christ. Our values, and this is not fancy —I'm going to share them with you in the rawest form so you will fully understand them—we value a move of God, being kind to one another, team ministry, fellowship, and doctrine."

"It's important," continued Pastor Chambers, "that you don't just pick random values to create a value statement. Such efforts are a waste of time. Instead, consider this: Your behaviors reveal your values. You can say you believe in the importance of such-and-such, but if you aren't doing such-and-such, then you don't really value it. Values are always revealed by observable behaviors.

"Interestingly, the importance of a person's behaviors is revealed in Scripture. 'Whatever you sow, that shall you also reap.' Behaviors will always result in a destination. So if you don't like the direction you're headed in, change your behaviors. But before you change your behaviors, you have to address your values—because values are what drive behavior."

Jon was jotting more notes than he had on any of his previous visits. He wrote, "Values drive behavior," and circled the phrase to highlight its importance. When he finished writing he remarked, "Wow, this is good. I can see where I need to go back and take our team through this. It's one thing to have a purpose, but it's another to know how you're going to accomplish it. And values are the root or foundation of the *how*."

"That's correct," Pastor Chambers agreed.

"I'm sorry if my questions make it sound like I'm not getting it," said Jon, "but I don't want to miss anything. Exactly how then does the Pentecostals of Tri-Cities live out . . ." he paused to glance at his notes . . . "a move of God, being kind to one another, team ministry, fellowship, and doctrine?"

"That's a good question," said Pastor Chambers. "While this may sound as if I'm oversimplifying it, our team has created virtue statements, which are simple sentences that help people understand how we are aligned with our values."

"Can you give me an example?" asked Jon.

"Sure. For instance, 'Because we value fellowship, we connect with others outside of our church services.' Or 'Because we value being kind to one another, we will be quick to give each other the benefit of the doubt.' Or 'Because we value team ministry, we will outdo one another in showing honor.'"

"Oh, I see," said Jon. "I like that."

"We have several such virtue statements for each of our core values," continued Pastor Chambers. "We want everyone to know that our values are not meaningless words. We live by them, and this is how we do it." Then he added, "It also helps people translate a concept into an action."

"Here's another question," said Jon. "How do we identify our values? Should I just borrow yours?" He laughed.

Smiling, Pastor Chambers said, "I wouldn't suggest that. To a large extent, the core values of the church will flow out of your heart and out of the heart of your core leaders. God has had you on a journey for a long time. You've experienced some things that have helped shape you—the way you act, the way you think. The same is true for your wife and your leadership team. Those things have helped to shape your values."

Pastor Chambers leaned toward Jon. "You could start by asking yourself, 'What are those lessons? What are the things that I feel most drawn to? What are the things that are most important to me?' Those things— the things you value the most—are your values. It isn't a wish list or a fanciful sound bite. They are what you truly believe in. Those are the things you believe are most needed to get to where you want to go. And the purpose of identifying those values is so that everyone will orbit around them. This is the *how* to your *why*."

Jon asked, "But what if the things I'm believing in . . . the things I value . . . are not the right things? What if I've had an experience, and the lesson I've drawn from it isn't what I should have learned? For instance, what if I was hurt at some point in my life and the lesson or the values I now have cause me to never let myself get close to anyone again? Wouldn't that be a bad thing?" asked Jon.

"Yes, it would," said Pastor Chambers. "That's why you must always view your values in light of the Word of God. God's Word trumps everything else."

"Amen to that," said Jon. "I guess this is part of that 'helping others grow' that you're always emphasizing."

"That's right," said Pastor Chambers. "Helping others grow involves confronting wrong values. That's exactly what Jesus did. Consider when He confronted

Peter, calling him Satan. That had to do with Peter's values. He was valuing self over the Father's purpose.

"Or consider the disciples who were vying for a position of prominence, wanting to sit on Jesus' right hand or left hand. They were displaying a wrong set of values while Jesus was always calling His disciples to align with Kingdom values.

"I especially love how, in His restoration of Peter, Jesus focused on values. He asked, 'Do you love Me, Peter?' Jesus asked him three times, and each time followed it up with a virtue statement: 'Then feed my sheep.'"

"Oh, I get it!" exclaimed Jon. "That's the 'chair principle.'"

Pastor Chambers smiled and said, "That's correct."

"Let me ask you another question," said Jon. "You say that you value a move of God. How does valuing a move of God help you fulfill your purpose of making disciples? Or how does being kind to one another help you fulfill your purpose?"

"Great question," said Pastor Chambers. "Let's look at it. Consider the value of a move of God. It's impossible for someone to become a disciple without having an experience; God has to be more to someone than mere head knowledge."

"Yes," interrupted Jon, "that one is fairly easy. But how does 'being kind' help you fulfill your purpose for example?"

Pastor Chambers replied, "The Bible says, 'By this shall all men know you are my disciples.'"

"Well, yeah, that's easy too," said Jon, interrupting before Pastor Chambers could finish his remarks.

Laughing, Pastor Chambers said, "You're the one who asked about it."

Jon rushed on, "How about teamwork? How does the value of teamwork help the Pentecostals of Tri-Cities fulfill its purpose?"

"Jesus discipled His disciples in a team context. That's just one of many examples I could give."

Pastor Jon laughed. "I guess I was just overthinking the issue. This all makes perfect sense. Thank you for bearing with me."

Pastor Chambers said, "It's one of our values . . . being kind," to which both men laughed.

"Are you ready to go eat?" asked Pastor Chambers.

"I can definitely eat," said Jon with a smile.

"We aren't far from the restaurant," said Pastor Chambers. "I need to make a phone call and get some gas. So let me do that, and I'll meet you there . . . let's say . . . in twenty minutes? That should give me enough time."

"That's perfect," said Jon. "That should give me enough time to finish my notes."

"Okay. See you in twenty minutes," said Pastor Chambers as he headed out the door.

A Conversation of Three

When Jon entered the restaurant, Pastor Chambers was already seated and actively talking and laughing with someone at the table. Seeing Jon, Pastor Chambers motioned him over.

"Pastor Jon, I want you to meet a close friend of mine. This is William Barnes. William, this is Pastor Jon, my friend I was telling you about."

"It's good to meet you," said William, shaking Jon's hand.

"The same," said Jon cordially.

"William is going to join us for lunch," said Pastor Chambers. "I said nothing about it before because I wasn't sure it was going to work out until I called him right after I left the coffeehouse. William and I grew up together in Wisconsin, and here we are all of these years later, living just a couple of hours away from one another. We try to meet up as much as possible, which isn't as much as we would like."

"That's for sure," said William. "But we always have a good time when we do."

"I invited William for lunch because I wanted you to meet him, largely because of our subject today. William has some insight that helped me some years ago, and I thought it would be great if you could hear it from the expert."

"Oh, I wouldn't describe myself as an expert," said William, "but I will do my best."

"I look forward to hearing it," said Jon.

Pastor Chambers explained, "Pastor Jon and I have been meeting about once a month for the past six months. I've been sharing with him how to overcome growth inhibitors. We've been having a great time meeting up, and I have even gotten him into fly-fishing."

"Oh no, not fly-fishing," said William, smiling from ear to ear. He turned to Jon. "He started fly-fishing as a last resort because he couldn't beat me at golf." The men shared a laugh.

After the men had ordered their meals, William said, "I don't know if my good friend here has shared anything about me or what I do, but I'm a college track coach."

"This is a first for me," said Jon. "I've never met or talked with a track coach."

"He's being modest," said Pastor Chambers. "He isn't just a college track coach; he's one of the best. He coaches world-class runners and is an author of a best-selling book about how anyone can achieve optimal performance."

"Impressive," said Jon. "I'm sure there's much I could learn from you. I've always been fascinated with marathon runners, but I know little about the sport. Just that they must have incredible endurance."

"That's true," said William.

Pastor Chamber said, "I invited William to meet us for lunch primarily because I wanted you to hear his insight into performance versus values. It's very important in light of what we've been talking about today."

"What Chambers is referring to," said William, "is something I had to learn the hard way. I was quite the runner when I was young. Ran in college. Set numerous records and had a bright future in front of me, including the Olympics and so on. Then I experienced burnout. I crashed. And that was the end of that. I walked away from running and wanted nothing more to do with it.

"A few years went by, and I was struggling to make ends meet . . . newly married with our first child on the way. Someone reached out to me and asked me to coach them. I had been turning offers down, but times were so tough that I relented and said yes. And here I am today, nearly twenty-seven years later.

"Once I started coaching it didn't take long before the joy of running returned. Looking back at the time that I quit running, I noticed that a diminishing of the joy of running preceded the burnout I experienced. I then analyzed what had caused my joy of running to diminish, and I discovered the answer. The rest is history. It wasn't long before I was coaching world-class runners, then writing a book, and so on."

With that, he paused.

"What was it that caused the diminishing of your joy of running?" Jon asked, leaning in.

"Let me start by saying that purpose is different than performance. I had become so consumed with performance that I wasn't aligned with my purpose."

Jon sat in silence at this revelation. *Am I consumed with performance?* he wondered. *Or am I aligned with my purpose? What are my core values?*

Pastor Chambers looked at Jon and said, "This is something I believe ministers need to hear. And I will go even a step further: I believe our churches are full of people—businessowners, fathers, mothers, young men and women, and so on—who need to hear this. It's the difference between living with joy or living without it," he added.

"He's right," said William. "Performance-driven people are always pushing, driving, trying to attain, but they never seem to get what they're chasing after." He paused and then said, "I used to be that person. I was winning races, setting records, and becoming a household name within the running circles, but I felt empty. It was kind of crazy. Here I was longing for something but wasn't sure what I was longing for. I had fallen into a trap. I was consumed with impressing people, and it was getting me nowhere.

"I could win a race or set a record, and everyone applauded me for it. Everything looked good on the outside, and I was okay with that. It kept everyone at a distance so to speak—kept everyone from seeing the real me. Instead, people saw the revised version of me.

The winner version. The record-holder version. But not the real version of me.

"It became like a drug. I was addicted. Sure, it was fun for a while. I was highly motivated to keep it that way, to stay on top, to beat everyone around me. My performance was my everything. Things are different nowadays. I now want to impact people. There's a big difference."

Jon scribbled in his notebook: "I want to impact people, not impress people."

William talked on: "The first sign of an impending crash was when it started dawning on me that there wasn't much more for me to do. I was nearing the top of my profession. 'What then?' I asked myself. 'What will I do after this?'

"It was about a year and a half later that I experienced burnout. There's a lot to that part of the story that I'll skip, but let's just say it was a very hard time. But here is the good news: I'm on the other side of things now. And I absolutely love what I do. I'm in constant contact with people I care about, and they care about me. I'm not afraid to show my vulnerability, as you can see by me having this conversation with you, someone I just met. It is kind of crazy . . . the more vulnerable I allow myself to be, the more aligned I become with my purpose."

William continued, "Here's what I finally realized, and perhaps this will sum it up: When it is all said and done, I don't want to be remembered for the records I set. I want to be remembered for the lives I've changed for the better. You don't change lives by setting records. You don't change lives through your performance. You change lives when you align with your purpose."

"That's good," said Jon, while making yet another note: "Performance doesn't change lives; lives are changed when we align with our purpose."

"Unfortunately," said William, "most people are performance driven. Most people are trying to impress other people. Your greatest impact on others doesn't happen through a performance; it happens when you are aligned with your purpose.

"Consider this," he continued. "When you pass away . . . when all is said and done . . . what will people say when standing by your casket? Will they tell stories of servitude, of time spent with them, of the time you lent a listening ear, of moments of heart connection? Or will they talk about how polished you were in the pulpit? Will they talk about all of your accomplishments? What is it about your life that is impacting people the most?"

Without waiting for a response from Jon, William continued, "The truest treasures in life are closely connected with heartbeats—with people, not records or accomplishments. Yet most people are chasing after accomplishments.

"Yes, I set many records. I became a household name. To a certain extent, even now, within my circle of coaching, I'm a household name. But when it is all said and done, my goals, the things I'm passionate about, are not performance oriented. I want to make a positive impact on those around me. And that, as crazy as it may sound, has elevated me to the top of my field—not my abilities.

"I see this all the time with church leaders," William continued. "They get it backwards. Many are trying to build churches rather than build people. I see it with business owners too. People are your greatest asset."

"That's what Pastor Chambers says!" exclaimed Jon. "You're a track coach, but are you sure you aren't a preacher too?"

"I'm sure," William replied, laughing. "I do, however, speak some at my church."

"I'm not surprised at that," said Jon. "You know what you need to do? You need to host coaching sessions for pastors. Church leaders all over need to hear this. It's outstanding."

Smiling, William said, "Well, to a certain extent, I do have coaching sessions with preachers."

It suddenly dawned on Jon that William was referencing the conversation the two were having at the moment. He wondered, but didn't ask, how many such conversations William had conducted with others like him.

Jon spoke up, "So help me understand something, William. How does all of this . . . being purpose driven instead of performance driven . . . relate with core values?"

"Good question," replied William. "It has everything to do with it. Values are the *how* one fulfills one's purpose. If your *how* points to performance, then you probably need to look closely at whether you are truly fulfilling your purpose. You are likely misaligned. You are probably trying to impress others rather than impact others. If, however, your *how* points to impacting others, then you are likely aligned with your purpose."

Jon was busy taking notes. He knew this was something he wanted to refer to again and again. He knew it would take some time before he fully assimilated it. *The good thing is,* he thought, *I'm surrounded by some people who get it. They will help me. It's what they value too.*

123

Home

An hour later Jon was on his way home. Driving down the interstate, he rehearsed the day's conversation over and over in his mind.

Am I performance driven or purpose driven? he asked himself.

He concluded that he displayed signs of both, with perhaps a little more emphasis on performance than he would have liked. He recognized that his tendencies to be performance driven could be seen in the emphasis he placed on various aspects of the church and his own ministry. He had to admit that much of what he did was aimed at trying to impress others.

But isn't it for a good purpose? he thought. *After all, I'm trying to build a church.*

Then he immediately thought, *But is that what I'm supposed to be doing? Shouldn't I be centered on impacting people? Isn't that my calling? To equip others, to disciple people? If so, I should be more purpose driven than performance driven.*

He then asked himself, *What if I used performance to make disciples, wouldn't that be okay?*

As soon as the question formed in his mind, he rejected it with a memory of something William had said, at least in so many words: "You can't fully impact others with performance. You can impress them, but not fully impact them."

It would take some time for Jon to fully understand it all and align with it, but he was determined to overcome growth inhibitors. His core values were being altered for the better. Authenticity, vulnerability, allowing others to draw close, and so on, were becoming increasingly important.

And isn't that how disciples are made, Jon thought.

The Application

OVERVIEW

Overcoming church growth barriers is a common concept within church circles. (Notice the use of the word *barriers*.) Multiple books have been written on the subject, and many seminars and conferences have addressed it. Much of the material is beneficial.

For example, consider the number of available parking spots or the seating capacity of a sanctuary. The general rule of thumb is that a church will not grow beyond 80 percent of its capacity. These things and more are important and should be considered.

That is not, however, what this book is about. Instead of focusing on church growth, this book is about overcoming obstacles that hinder the growth of people. The underlying premise is that churches thrive when the growth of people results in the growth of a church.

Additionally, this book is written on the premise that the fivefold ministry's calling is to equip people for the work of their ministry (Ephesians 4:11–12). Hence, the emphasis is on overcoming things that inhibit people from fulfilling God's call on their lives. It's on helping people grow a church leader's God-given purpose.

The Background of This Story

Much of the fable stemmed from my own story. In many ways, I was Jon. I was a young pastor struggling to find the answer to church growth. It was during this time that a pastor several years older befriended me. Often while attending special meetings, he would invite me to join him for dinner and fellowship. Some years later he asked me to join his ministerial staff as the family pastor. I will be forever grateful for his investment in my development.

A couple years after joining the ministerial staff, he asked me if I had been able to identify a few principles that I hadn't seen before, things that if I had it to do all over again (serve as senior pastor), I would do differently now. I quickly responded with a list of five things. Many of the principles in this book can be seen in that list of five principles I shared with him, things I had witnessed in a local context as being a part of the ministerial team. And a few of them are identical to what I said in this book.

Additionally, several of the stories are similar or rooted in actual occasions that occurred during the nine years I served on the pastoral staff. The church was a growing, thriving congregation of over six hundred.

After resigning and moving to another state, we based out of another growing, thriving congregation for eighteen months. This congregation consisted of over one thousand members. I was privileged to sit in on many staff meetings, forge close friendships with several members of the ministerial team, and learn much from them. Unsurprisingly, I witnessed much of the same principles at work in this assembly as I had in the previous one.

I was then asked to come on staff at yet another growing, thriving congregation, this time as executive pastor. Once again, as in the previous two churches, I witnessed the same principles being applied as well as having a close friendship with the senior pastor and other ministerial leaders in the church.

My first experience in ministry came from my home church pastored by my father. After graduating from Bible college, I assisted my father for nine years, first as youth pastor and later as associate pastor. While the church was small in number of attendees, the lessons learned were of no less importance. Some of those lessons are sprinkled throughout the fable. Additionally, my father-in-law, a writer and pastor, has greatly impacted my thinking.

Hence, the stories and principles found throughout this book stem from a variety of fronts: from being a senior pastor of a small fledging church to serving on the pastoral team of large-size congregations, from ministering in North America to being involved in ministerial efforts abroad. Numerous friends and mentors also have had a positive impact on my life, some of which is reflected in various stories throughout the fable.

To all, I am forever grateful.

Such is the background of this story.

The Five Growth Inhibitors

The fable addresses five inhibitors to the growth of people, and ultimately, the growth of a church. These growth inhibitors are shared in the story as action statements.

If you don't invite others to the table, they won't fully engage.

If you don't celebrate others for who they are, you are simply using them.

If you don't allow structure to evolve, it becomes a lid.

If you don't orbit around a worthy and compelling cause, self-interest will rule.

If you focus on performance instead of values, you will impress but not impact.

These action statements address key issues as to why the growth of people is often stunted. Consider the following:

Apathy: *If you don't invite others to the table, they won't fully engage.*

Misalignment: *If you don't celebrate others for who they are, you are simply using them.*

Restricted environment: *If you don't allow structure to evolve, it becomes a lid.*

Self-interest: *If you don't orbit around a worthy and compelling cause, self-interest will rule.*

Disingenuousness: *If you focus on performance instead of values, you will impress but not impact.*

The succeeding chapters of this book take an even closer look at each growth inhibitor and offer clear steps in how to overcome them.

ENGAGEMENT

*If you don't invite others to the table,
they won't fully engage.*

Paul wrote in Titus 2:14 that we are to be zealous or impassioned about good works. But church leaders often don't witness this as they survey the congregation. Some people are growing, but many are not—at least not in a zealous or enthusiastic way. The struggle, then, comes not in our knowledge of this problem but in knowing what to do about it.

Unfortunately, regardless of the efforts of church leaders to combat apathy by promoting such things as revival services, prayer and fasting, special events, and so on, apathy still abounds. At times the various efforts of church leaders will prove beneficial, but in most cases, it isn't long before things revert to the way they used to be. When we stop and think about it, it makes us ponder if what we witnessed (an increase of good works) flowed from deep within or if it was merely floating on the surface.

Thank God, we think, *for those who are deeply committed. Without such people, we would truly be in a mess.* On average the majority of church leaders would attest that approximately 20 percent of the congregation is deeply committed. Such people, we think, are zealous for good works. With them, apathy is a non-issue. But that is not necessarily true. It is not just those who are spiritually lethargic—preoccupied with the lesser things of life—who battle apathy. Their condition is obvious. However, apathy also exists among those who are dedicated and deeply committed, perhaps not in observable ways, but apathy exists nonetheless.

Perhaps you're thinking it's impossible for a person who is zealous for good works to battle apathy. Consider this: Apathy exists among the deeply committed when they offer less than they could. Less energy. Less zeal. Less of themselves, their talents, their passions, their giftings, and their abilities. It is this "less than they could be" that qualifies as apathy. It is this understanding of apathy that enables one to attest to the fact that it abounds even among the deeply committed.

Why the focus on apathy among the deeply committed 20 percent of the congregation? Consider the 80/20 rule, also known as the Pareto Principle. When applied within the context of a local church, the 80/20 rule suggests that church leadership should place the bulk of its energy and focus on 20 percent of the congregation—the 20 percent who are deeply committed and zealous for good works. It is these people who have the greatest impact on a congregation.

Stated yet another way, if a church leader can figure out how to help the deeply committed overcome apathy, we can apply the same principle to the other 80 percent. And who will have the most impact on the 80 percent? The top 20 percent. Once you lead the deeply committed to overcoming apathy, they will lead the others to overcome it too.

So exactly how do church leaders lead others to overcome apathy and forge ahead to growth? The brief answer is that people tend to grow and learn when they are engaged in doing something. This is important for church leaders to remember. People don't grow merely by hearing; people grow as they move from hearing to doing.

Consider research conducted during the 1960s by Edgar Dale, an American educator. He developed what is known as Dale's Cone of Experience. Dale theorized that people learn more by what they *do* as opposed to what they *hear, read,* or *see.* And his research proved his assumptions correct. Specifically, he discovered people generally remember only 10 percent of what they read, 20 percent of what they hear, 30 percent of what they see, 50 percent of what they see and hear, 70 percent of what they say and write, and 90 percent of what they do.

Church leaders can benefit from Dale's research. When leaders invite people to the table, they (1) help others overcome apathy and (2) give them an opportunity to grow. But that's not all. When people are allowed to be part of what happens at the table, buy-in is generated.

My Story

One difficulty in my transition from being the senior pastor to assuming the role and responsibility as the family pastor was the thought that I would simply implement another man's vision. Being a visionary, this wasn't an easy thing for me to do.

I vividly recall, however, a conversation that occurred a few months after we arrived. The senior pastor asked me, "What is your vision for family ministries?" I replied, as I thought I should, "What is your vision? I will make it happen." He then said, "I appreciate that. But I would like to hear your vision." I refused to budge. I believed, as I had often heard it said, that the senior pastor has the vision, and everyone else should seek to make it happen.

He finally relented, saying, "My vision is to start family ministries and bring Eugene and Kerri Wilson here to be the family pastor. Now what is your vision for family ministries?" As I write these words, I am deeply moved by his words and actions. He invited me, a visionary, to the table. He allowed me to have a voice. And I became fully engaged and zealous for good works because of it.

Empowering Others

Pastor Chambers states in the fable, "Inviting people to the table is about helping people grow and releasing them to function in their God-given talents and abilities and callings. By allowing them to contribute— empowering people to help design and create and build and develop processes and ministries—we are removing growth inhibitors in their lives."

Let's change the sentence somewhat while stating the same thing: When you empower people to function within their abilities and callings, you help people grow. The question, therefore, is what does it mean to empower someone else? Many things could be said in response, but here are just a few:

1. It means you will need to step back so they can step forward.
2. It means you are going to allow others to make key decisions, or at the minimum, you will take into serious consideration opinions that differ from your own.
3. It means you will allow others to dream and then lend verbal support and offer resources to accomplish that dream.
4. It means you will allow others to be an integral part of things, including being open with communication in areas that matter.

In contrast, people who aren't invited to the table—who don't feel empowered, who aren't asked to take part in meaningful conversation—will not engage. They will put forth less-than-ideal effort. The latter happens more often than many church leaders recognize.

Let's take a closer look at less-than-ideal effort. One reason people battle apathy is because of the lack of involvement with things they are passionate about. This could be true for both the deeply committed and the spiritually lethargic. One question we should ask is, "Why aren't people engaged in doing what they are passionate about?" Sometimes it's because we haven't given people the opportunity to explore, to discover their passion. At other times, the opportunity exists, but because there is no invitation, people don't step forward. This is especially true for those who lack an assertive personality.

The biggest hurdle, however, isn't a lack of opportunity. In most churches, opportunities for ministry involvement abound. Perhaps this is why church leaders struggle in understanding how even the deeply committed may not be fulfilling their passion.

There is an abundance of ministry opportunities, church leaders think. *What's stopping people from getting involved in the things they are passionate about?* It is true there are many ministry opportunities. And yes, as church leaders we commonly do our best to plug people in. But delegating tasks and fitting "round" people into our square pegs, so to speak, is a far cry from empowering someone.

The difference between delegation and empowerment can often be found in our answer to the underlying purpose of ministry—are we trying to grow the church or grow people? We often create ministries and then assign people to those ministries in attempts to grow the church. In contrast, we are more likely to empower people when the goal is to help people grow.

Last, another reason apathy might exist among the deeply committed is due to disillusionment. According to *Oxford Languages,* disillusionment is defined as "a feeling of disappointment resulting from the discovery that something is not as good as one believed it to be." Unfortunately, this sentiment occurs from time to time as people who once thought their passions could be lived out within a local church discover that for whatever reason it doesn't appear so. Perhaps it is the lack of resources with a church, such as money or personnel. It could also be a timing factor or a lack of vision by senior leadership. The possibilities are many.

Engage the Disengaged

As church leaders, we want people to engage. We expect to see their passion and zeal on display in such things as their response in worship, to the Word of God, and through giving. While there is certainly nothing wrong with such expectations, what about areas that are not so readily seen? The point is simple—there is much more to passion and zeal than what occurs at church. Consider the public school teacher who extends hope to a student, or the saint who is caring for an ailing neighbor, or the woman who is thrilled to volunteer to help create designs for a nonprofit, and so on.

We also can be guilty of focusing on the results rather than the causes. For example, prayer, worship, and Bible study are all very important elements of a growing Christian's walk with God. When these things are lacking, we are concerned, and rightfully so. Apathetic people need to pray. They need to worship. They need to read the Word of God. But telling them what they need or ought to do is seldom highly effective. They already know they need to do such things.

Instead, ask yourself the question: What could I do that would cause a person to want to pray, read the Bible, or fast? Just as Pastor Chambers asked Jon if he found it easier to pray more when he was scheduled to speak, people will find it easier to be zealous when they're involved in something of significance. The way to engage them in discovering significance is by inviting them to the table.

DIVERSITY

*If you don't celebrate others for who they are,
you are simply using them.*

No two leaves of a tree are exactly alike. No two
snowflakes or fingerprints are the same. Neither are
people precisely identical. Differences in personalities,
talents, gifts, worldviews, experiences, and so on make
each of us unique.

Such differences should be celebrated, but this is
not always the case. In an attempt to create so-called
unity, some believe others should think as they think,
act as they act, respond as they would respond, and so
on. While there is certainly room for development, as
leaders, we should never feel that everyone should do
things exactly as we would do them.

It is important that we strive to maintain the unity of
the Spirit. Paul wrote in Ephesians 4:3, "Endeavouring
to keep the unity of the Spirit in the bond of peace."

This commitment requires effort, especially with those who think or do things differently than you or I would do them. Unity, however, is possible because of our diversity—not despite our diversity.

Although from time to time we struggle with keeping "the unity of the Spirit," it should not diminish the value and importance of our diversity. Paul wrote about "diversities of gifts" (I Corinthians 12:4), "differences of administrations" (I Corinthians 12:5), and "diversities of operations" (I Corinthians 12:6). He maintained that differences should be valued and appreciated, that no one within the body should look down on others who have different gifts, and no one should strive to be something he or she is not called to be (I Corinthians 12:15–26).

Interestingly, earlier in his letter, Paul said that some within the church were saying, "I am of Paul." Others were saying, "I am of Apollos." Still others were saying, "I am of Cephas" (Peter). Paul addressed the situation head-on. He said such talk was wrong and asked why they were dividing the body of Christ. He added they were acting like spoiled children who could therefore handle only the "milk of the word" rather than "strong meat," which was spiritual food for the spiritually mature (I Corinthians 3:1–2).

One might think, based on Paul's words, he was speaking against diversity. If so, one would be mistaken. In I Corinthians 4:7, he asked his readers this question: "For who maketh thee to differ from another? and what hast thou that thou didst not receive?" Although there were factions within the church, Paul did not speak against distinctions or differences. Instead, he said, "Don't you know God made all of you different and that everything you have in talents and capabilities was a gift from God?"

Paul and Apollos and Peter were created in different molds with different talents to accomplish different missions. Therefore, to divide over them, to create factions within the church, was evidence of spiritual immaturity. Paul was saying it is wrong to side with one specific personality or talent or gifting. Instead, the spiritually mature value and appreciate differences.

I have attempted to establish a scriptural principle for celebrating people for who they are as opposed to simply using them. Jesus shared a parable that points to the fact that God has given "to every man his work" (Mark 13:34), as well as the ability to perform it. Paul wrote that the Holy Spirit distributes gifts "to every man severally as he will" (I Corinthians 12:11). I am convinced that if every member would fulfill the mission God has appointed him or her to fulfill, there would be no jealousy or divisions. No two persons would ever do the same thing in the same way. This might be the challenge for us as church leaders—not only allowing people to do things differently than we would do them, but also celebrating those differences.

Several Ways to Do Things

Of the various differences between people (worldviews, experiences, and so on) personality differences are likely the most obvious. Some people are big picture while others focus on details. Some are people-oriented while others are task-oriented. All are a blend of varying amounts of these traits or tendencies.

While personality assessments offer many benefits, some of which are described in the fable, there are a few things to note. First, no one personality trait is better than another. The healthiest teams comprise all types. Second, no one should use personality deficiencies as an excuse to act in ungodly ways that violate the core values of an organization or team. Third, no one wants to be labeled or placed within a box based on a personality assessment. I don't blame them. There is more to a person than what personality assessments reveal. Our experiences, worldviews, values, and so on shape and influence much of what we do. This is not to say, however, that personality assessments hold no value, for indeed they do.

Most of us would acknowledge we are different and that we appreciate people for who they are. But what we know to be true in our mind isn't always displayed in our actions. We often believe if people would do things the way we do them, think as we think, see things the way we see them, and so on, things would be much better. Consider time consciousness. If everyone were as time conscious as I am (or maybe the opposite depending on your point of view), things would be much better. How about worship styles? If people would just "get with it," or if so-and-so would stop all the nonsense movement, things would be much better. The possibilities are endless.

Letting Others Shine

We may struggle in seeing it, but we often say one thing and believe another. We often use Scripture to back our feelings concerning what are simply differences in our personalities. Hence, we set out on an endeavor to "fix" others. But our fixing others is often nothing more than endeavoring to make carbon copies of ourselves. One of my friends did this. He told me of a time when he was trying to "fix" his assistant. He said the Lord spoke to him and asked him what he was doing. He explained, "Lord, I'm trying to help Jack grow." The Lord replied, "No, you're not. You're trying to make him like you."

Not that people don't want to grow, for indeed they do. But people also want to be valued and accepted. Our helping others grow should mean that we allow others to shine in their distinct personality, calling, and gifting; it should mean that they understand we value and appreciate them, their personality, their gifting, their calling, and so on.

Jesus worked with an array of personality types. One cannot deny the varying differences among the disciples. It is clear they were different. Understanding their differences, Jesus said, "By this shall all men know that ye are my disciples, if ye have love one to another" (John 13:35). Have you ever considered the thought that our appreciation of one another, celebrating our differences, is a distinction? It is what sets us apart from the world.

If you want to appreciate others, including personality differences and callings, rather than simply using them, ask them:
- What has God called you to do?
- What do you feel is your spiritual gifting?
- What is your personality blend? Have you ever taken a personality assessment?
- In what areas do you and I (or others on the team) complement you or frustrate you?
- Where do you feel you are on your spiritual journey, and have you identified your next step?
- Do you understand your strengths and weaknesses?

- How might I help you with any of the afore-mentioned questions?

As church leaders, it is important that we help others develop, that we help our teams grow, and that we endeavor to maintain the unity of the Spirit. One way we do this is by gaining an understanding and appreciation of our differences.

This endeavor—understanding and appreciating one another—helps us overcome the common growth inhibitor—the lack of diversity. The lack of diversity in churches is more common than many readily recognize. It happens when we attempt to plug people into serving without truly considering both their natural and their God-given personalities, callings, talents, and gifts. It happens as we celebrate giftings and personality traits that are similar to ours and shun all others. It occurs when we hold back others who just don't seem to think as we think.

Hence, while we may use such people, we will not release them to be who they really are. As church leaders, we should never want to just use people; we should desire to help people function in their God-given calling and do so in the way God made them to be.

We Often Want to Be Apollos

Not only should we celebrate and appreciate others for whom God made them to be, we also should celebrate whom God made us to be.

Unfortunately, some church leaders struggle being whom God made them to be. Most of us admire those who can "wax elegant" like Apollos. Let's be honest. Who wouldn't like to wow the crowds, to be able to frame our words and shape our delivery in the way Apollos did? But not everyone is called to be Apollos.

In fact, there has been only one. Likewise, there is only one you.

What about Paul? Most of us likely would admit we would love to make a difference as Paul did. But how many of us would embrace his way of speaking? Few, if any, I would surmise. A present-day Paul would never be asked to preach at a conference. Yet Paul had a greater impact on the early church than anyone else. The point is simple: we often gravitate to a particular style or a particular personality rather than celebrating one another's differences.

Celebrating differences shouldn't mean we attempt to become a carbon copy of someone else. Young preachers should never attempt to emulate older ministers they admire in order to become like them; first, such a thing would be impossible, and second, doing so would be contrary to the plan of God. Each person should be himself and himself only.

Last, a final word of caution: Although we should celebrate our differences, we should never place ourselves at the center. Every preacher must preach according to his personality, but he must be careful not to "preach his personality." Ultimately, it isn't about one's personality; it's about the God who gave it to us.

STRUCTURE

*If you don't allow structure to evolve,
it becomes a lid.*

When evaluating the success of an organization, special emphasis is usually placed on strategy while organizational design and structure are often viewed as an afterthought. This is true with churches and church leaders as well. When seeking to understand why a church is experiencing church growth, most look at its strategies. Few consider the value of its organizational structure. The role that organizational design and structure plays in creating growth, however, is undeniable. Furthermore, it can be seen in Scripture.

Consider the early church. The church sought only as much structure as it needed to move its mission forward. For example, when it came time to replace Judas, instead of adding both Barsabas and Matthias, they decided to add Matthias only. The existing structure remained unchanged until Acts 6, when some Greek-speaking Jews within the church spoke out concerning the daily distribution of goods, saying some widows were not receiving as much assistance as others. Although prejudicial feelings probably had something to do with it, the disciples also recognized they were partly to blame. They were too busy to handle the needs of the burgeoning congregation.

Although the existing structure had been instituted by Jesus Himself, change was needed to keep up with the demands of a growing church. The current structure was no longer sufficient to fulfill a crucial element in its body care. This is not to say, however, that there was anything wrong with its structure early on. It had worked for a time. They had fulfilled the purpose to go forth and impact the world. But the church's ability to achieve success was being diminished because of the lack of changes in organizational structure. Thus, when the changes were made in Acts 6, great things happened. The church experienced even greater growth!

Defining Organizational Structure

What exactly is organizational structure? Organizational structure is about coordinating an organization's activities. It is how the people and teams within the organization link together to accomplish the overarching purpose. A well-designed structure allows individuals and teams within an organization to communicate effectively, synergize, strategize, and so on, to best achieve the organization's goals and objectives. Consequently, structure greatly impacts an organization's ability to achieve success.

Unfortunately, some church leaders are resistant to learning about or working with structure. Some say that an emphasis on structure seems too "businesslike" or "formal" because the church is supposed to be a spiritual family. Such thinking, however, often fails to consider that Jesus had a core team of three, a committed team of twelve, sent many other disciples out in pairs of two, and so on.

Many of the issues church leaders deal with could be best addressed through the implementation of structure, or changes to an existing one. A poor organizational structure causes a confusion of roles and responsibilities, lack of coordination with others, lack of communication, a failure to share ideas, and unneeded stress and conflict.

Often when an organization grows, stress is placed on its current structure. Thus, an organization's structure should be in flux, changing to accommodate growth. When things that once worked well don't work so well anymore, consider the benefit of changing the current structure. While change is seldom easy or eagerly sought after, it is often necessary. At such times it is important to remember the overarching purpose.

According to Acts 1:8, the church was given the task or purpose of sharing the message of Jesus Christ with the world. This endeavor entailed such things as witnessing, fundraising (giving), preserving the doctrine, and connecting a geographically separated church. Furthermore, the early church established a council in Jerusalem and an organizational structure that included presbyters, deacons, and so on, all with the central purpose of achieving optimal effectiveness in performing its mission.

Last, the structure of the early church was small scale but ever expanding. It was comprised, somewhat, of semi-autonomous works networked together while orbiting around the common purpose—to impact the world. The vision was a global counterculture impact, and its members were deeply committed, even willing to die for the cause.

Types of Structure

The following is a brief overview of a few key elements regarding organizational structure and design within the church.

Centralization

In centralized organizations, those in top-level leadership make the decisions. In decentralized organizations, decisions are made and problems are solved by lower-level employees who are closer to the problem and have a better understanding of what to do. Neither centralization nor decentralization is necessarily bad or good. It all depends on the unique needs of the church and its culture.

Most churches tend to function as a centralized organization, as many churches are small in size. An additional factor that influences church leaders to lean toward centralization is the mindset that the pastor is in charge and responsible for leading the church. In such a pastor-centric model, the pastor must have the final say in all matters pertaining to the church, including but not limited to the building, decor (often coordinated by the pastor's wife), finances, and so on.

In contrast, large churches tend to function as decentralized organizations. While the senior pastor leads spiritually and has the final say with certain matters pertaining to the church, others are empowered to make decisions.

While some people only desire to serve—"just tell me what to do"—others desire to lead. This is not a negative. God wired them as such. Furthermore, if the church is to experience continual growth, leaders are needed. Hence, growing leaders is a necessity. One way people grow is by doing.

Now let's imagine you are a growing leader attending Pastor Chambers's church and you want to make a difference. You can envision things as they should be and understand how to work with others. Would you feel most comfortable being a leader in a decentralized church like Pastor Chambers's church? Or would you rather be a part of a centralized church in which senior-level leadership makes most of the decisions? If you are like most high-functioning leaders, the answer is obvious: you would choose a decentralized church. You are not alone.

Leaders who are growing are most likely to be attracted to senior-level church leaders who share power. When allowed to make decisions, people are able to stretch their abilities and experience growth. In contrast, centralized churches limit the growth of growing leaders by hoarding decision-making responsibilities.

The argument can be made, and many times rightfully so, that by holding on to decision-making authority, senior leaders can lessen the risk involved in making the wrong decision. But by not involving others, senior leaders thwart the growth of others. Therefore, the answer isn't one or the other (centralization or decentralization), but "both" and "and."

Formalization

Formalization is the extent to which an organization's policies, procedures, job descriptions, and rules are written and explicitly articulated. Many churches function with little formalization. Direction comes from the senior pastor and is seldom, if ever, in written form or policy. Larger churches tend to operate within a formalized structure with written rules and policies.

There are advantages to both formalized and unformalized structures within the church. Formalization provides direction. People know what to expect as the expectations are clearly stated. Too much formalization, however, can reduce innovation in that it can be too controlling, resulting in reduced motivation and a slower response time.

In the fable, Pastor Chambers's church had a higher level of formalization than Pastor Jon's church. While it might have been foolish in Pastor Jon's church to implement a high level of formalization, installing something as simple as job descriptions would be quite helpful, as was portrayed in the story.

Putting It into Action

Some common types of organizational structures include functional, divisional, flatarchy, and matrix structures. Rather than define each one, simply understand this—regardless of the type of structure, the purpose is to give a framework to how certain activities should be directed to achieve the organization's goals. It should provide some sense of direction on how the objectives of the organization can be accomplished.

The same is true for a church. A church's organizational structure defines how the activities of church members fit within the overall system. For example, in a centralized structure, the direction of a ministry comes primarily from the top; in a decentralized structure, various ministries within the church are given great leeway to decide what is best in achieving the overarching goal.

Senior leaders should consider the important role of structure in relationship to growth. A centralized structure enables the senior leadership to make the decisions. Hence, senior leadership does not have to concern itself with wondering what is happening. Control is held close. If other ministry leaders are afforded the opportunity to make decisions, the decisions made are generally presented to a senior-level leader (for example, the senior pastor or an assistant) for approval.

In contrast, in a decentralized structure, senior-level pastors empower others to make decisions, most of which do not have to cross the desk of senior-level leadership. For example, in a decentralized structure, senior-level leaders seldom bother themselves with decisions regarding church-building needs. This includes decorating, painting, repairs, and remodels. And neither does the senior pastor's wife, unless decorating is her gifting. Instead, others in the church who are gifted at such things are empowered to make the decisions. This is just one of many examples of what a decentralized structure within a church might look like.

The point is not to convince you, the reader, to let go of overseeing the physical aspects of a church, facilities, budgets, and so on. The point is that structure impacts growth; namely, the growth of people. Most often in a centralized structure the lid is senior-level leaders. Others are limited to implementation—putting into action what senior-level leaders have decided is best. In contrast, a decentralized structure empowers others to make decisions. With the lid removed, others are allowed to excel in their gifting. Unsurprisingly, buy-in is generated when others are given greater responsibilities.

Just Have Church

People think structure is "big church" stuff. But that's not true. Organizational structure existed in the efforts of Jesus and the twelve disciples. In addition, Jesus sending out the seventy in groups of two also is a form of organizational structure. The decision for church leaders isn't structure or no structure; the decision is whether to structure for growth or not to structure for growth. Church leaders who are interested in growth also are interested in understanding the importance of structure. It is not a "big church" thing; it is a growth thing.

Some might think, *All of this focus on organizational structure sounds too much like a business. The church is not a business; it's a body. We should just focus on having great church services.*

Such thinking isn't as sound as one might think. For example, healthy families maintain a sense of organizational structure. Parents commonly make the important decisions. Children are given responsibilities around the home that increase in importance as the children mature. In time, grown children move out on their own, starting the cycle over again. Likewise, healthy churches maintain a structure that enables growth, the growth of people. When others move on, it celebrates the growth that occurred while they were in the "household." It isn't viewed as a loss; it is viewed as an investment.

Job Descriptions

Just as structure shouldn't be viewed as a big-church thing, neither should job descriptions (often called ministry covenants). As was illustrated in the fable, job descriptions hold tremendous value for organizations of all types and sizes, including churches.

When it comes to church structure, job descriptions often are the missing link. Most churches in North America are small and do not necessarily need job descriptions to function. Most large-size churches, however, use job descriptions. The question is often, "Do I wait to install job descriptions until the church is a large church? Or should I use job descriptions now?" Based on what I have witnessed, one thing large churches do that enhances growth is to make use of job descriptions.

While much can be shared regarding job descriptions, some benefits of well-written job descriptions include the following:

Enable people to know the expectations

Empower people to make decisions within their area of responsibility

Clearly articulate the flow of communication

Help further develop people

Provide smooth transitions during changes of leadership

These are just a few of many benefits of working with job descriptions.

THE WHY

If you don't orbit around a worthy and compelling cause, self-interest will rule.

Haggai 1:6 describes what happens when one's priorities are skewed, when alignment with purpose has gone astray: "Ye have sown much, and bring in little; ye eat, but ye have not enough; ye drink, but ye are not filled with drink; ye clothe you, but there is none warm; and he that earneth wages earneth wages to put it into a bag with holes."

Haggai's message went forth about sixteen years after Cyrus decreed the Jews could return to Jerusalem from exile. According to Ezra 1:1–5, Cyrus allowed them to take the financial means and materials needed to rebuild the Temple. But upon their return to Judea, instead of engaging in what their hearts had yearned for, rebuilding the Temple, the people resorted to building a life for themselves.

It stands to reason that the first order of business would be to construct homes to live in while building the Temple. But that isn't exactly what the people did. Instead of building simple, ordinary houses, they constructed elaborate mansions—the most modern of the time. Although a decade and a half had passed since their return, they still hadn't gotten around to getting started on the Temple.

They said, "The time has not yet come to rebuild the house of the LORD" (Haggai 1:2, NLT). One might argue that time was needed to establish a supply of food. Seeds had to be sown and crops harvested. In addition, one might add the need for clothing. Such thinking seemed to rule the minds of the people. They planted crops. They made and bought fine clothing. Consequently, the people were living better than they'd ever lived before. They had more stuff, ate more, and were generally in much better shape than before.

Scripture, however, makes it clear—God had blessed them for a purpose. But instead of engaging in their God-given purpose, they gave themselves to the pursuit of prosperity. They ignored God's intention; they ignored the purpose of their return. The rebuilding of the Temple was to be their primary purpose. It was to be their first priority. But once they settled in Jerusalem, their priorities shifted.

So God spoke. He began by saying, "This people" (Haggai 1:2). This expression implies displeasure. God wasn't happy. After sixteen years the people were still saying, "The time has not yet come." Their objection was not to the rebuilding itself, but to the timing of it.

Perhaps the strongest argument for their failure to rebuild the Temple was that their efforts in getting ahead were not generating the expected return.

Although they were living a better lifestyle than ever, they were still lacking; they had sown much but were bringing in little compared to their efforts (Haggai 1:6). The root cause behind their economic and social hardship was misplaced priorities, a lack of alignment with their purpose.

Spiritual Leadership

Scripture is clear. The Lord wants His people to align with His will. We, His people, often struggle with doing so. We get caught up in matters that are not nearly as important as what we are called to do. We squander time; we waste potential. Our minds—thoughts and philosophies—reveal a tendency to be a little more like the world than we ought. We need our minds transformed (Romans 12:2), and this need highlights the importance of spiritual leaders.

In *Spiritual Leadership*, Henry and Richard Blackaby maintain that a spiritual leader is someone who, through influence, moves others away from self-agenda and toward God's agenda. Spiritual leaders help others adjust priorities; they help others align with their God-given purpose. Spiritual leaders hold great responsibility in establishing a culture of alignment with God's agenda. Spiritual leaders not only proclaim and explain Scripture, but they also live their lives as an example for others to follow.

Purpose matters a great deal. Interestingly, millennials and Gen Zs are highly motivated to improve society or the environment. If it is deemed morally good, a company's purpose can be a great connector with an increasingly large percentage of the population. Indeed, many people believe companies should be concerned with something more than just making money, that a company should be mission driven or morally aligned with a better society.

God's purpose, however, is greater than improving society or the environment. It is higher; it is more important. Ultimately, His plan encompasses a new earth. Adherence to His kingdom principles, as seen in the Beatitudes, would undoubtedly improve society. The point is simple: adherence to God's agenda ultimately generates what millennials and Gen Zs desire—an improved society and environment. Like the times of Haggai, however, efforts to improve things fall short when there is a lack of alignment with God's plan.

The Why

One struggle church leaders face in trying to influence others toward God's agenda is discovering and articulating a clear direction. The why isn't always as straightforward as we might think. In his book *Start with Why*, Simon Sinek stresses the importance of the why.

> We want to be around people and organizations who are like us and share our beliefs. When companies talk about WHAT they do and how advanced their products are, they may have appeal, but they do not necessarily represent something to which we want to belong. But when a company clearly communicates their WHY, what they believe, and we believe what they believe, then we will sometimes go to extraordinary lengths to include those products or brands in our lives.

As spiritual leaders, we must communicate the why to those we lead; the people must clearly understand the purpose. Why a particular ministry exists should be examined. If it is not fulfilling the overarching purpose of the church or if it is one of many ministries trying to accomplish a like purpose, we should consider whether the ministry should continue. Perhaps effort should be given to other areas that are lacking.

For example, years ago, the ministry I led within a local church hosted a fall festival. The purpose of the event was to connect with guests who had attended a recent service. Each year the church made special efforts to connect with the community on what we called Power Weekend. The highest attendance of the year was always on the Sunday of Power Weekend. Thousands of doorhangers, postcards, connect cards, and so on were distributed in the weeks leading up to Power Weekend.

We did a reasonably good job on the front end of Power Weekend (inviting people). And during Power Weekend, there was always a powerful move of the Lord with many people getting baptized and receiving the Holy Ghost. What we lacked was follow-up. After the event, we tended to return to life as usual. We sought to change that. We wanted something that would help the members of the church connect with the guests: thus the purpose of the fall outing.

The outing was a great success that first year. It was the largest fellowship gathering of the year. The attendees had a lot of fun—hayrides, smoked barbecue, bonfire for roasting marshmallows, games for kids. We erected a stage made of plywood on bales of hay inside of an old cotton gin. As I write, I do so with a smile as I think of all the fun we had.

But in the third year that event got moved because of so many other things going on at the church. So instead of it hosting it after Power Weekend, we held it before Power Weekend. Although most of the church members enjoyed the event, it was no longer meeting its purpose. The reason we started it in the first place was to connect with guests from Power Weekend. We had plenty of other fellowship events throughout the year; there was no need for another one, so the event was stopped.

Unfortunately, we failed to understand its value and its purpose. Other ministries were trying to fulfill their purpose(s). So while everyone enjoyed the event and wanted us to continue hosting it, no other church ministry offered to move dates or cancel an event(s) to accommodate the fall festival's original purpose. They were all trying to fulfill their own purpose(s).

This example is just one of many that showcase the struggle of alignment with purpose. Good things vie for our attention, sometimes causing our focus on the best things to wane. The struggle is real. We must home in on our why. Understanding our why is empowering. It enables us to do what we should and stop doing what we shouldn't. Clarity of purpose is the key.

Steve Jobs was known for saying no to lots of things so he could say yes to a few things. In fact, he was against Apple getting involved in making a phone until some others in the company convinced him it would be in essence like a minicomputer. The point is simple: understanding your why keeps you focused; it keeps you from being a jack-of-all-trades and a master of none.

You need to know your why. If you don't, you will find yourself caught up with things outside your purpose. This is a real issue for many church leaders. Too many are entangled with things outside of their purpose and so cannot fully engage with the most important things.

Helping others discover and align with God's distinct purpose in their hearts and lives is no simple task. Self-agenda gets in the way. Precious saints of God often struggle to align with God's specific purpose in their lives. Spiritual leaders are tasked with defining and articulating the "north star."

Practical Application

In practical terms, defining and articulating the north star involves mobilizing saints in ministry. Every saint, according to Scripture, has been gifted and called to ministry. The purpose of the fivefold ministry is to equip them for their ministry. We help others discover their why and engage in it.

It also involves helping others to understand they are not alone in their efforts. They are part of something much bigger than they may realize. Their role may seem small, but in reality, it is huge. Consider the parable of the three bricklayers. When a passerby asked each man what he was doing, the first man replied, "I'm laying bricks." The second man said, "I'm building a wall." The third man said proudly, "I'm building a cathedral." The critical role church leaders fulfill is in helping others understand and align with their why.

When people understand their why, they are better positioned to stay focused. Martha's life illustrates a person who is struggling with the why. She was "distracted." It wasn't that she was wrong in preparing a meal for her guest; she just wasn't aligned with the best thing. She wasn't aligned with the why. Consequently, she was "worried and upset about many things" (Luke 10:41).

In practical terms, it is vital leaders habitually start with the big rocks first. (For more information on this analogy, see Stephen Covey's "big rocks first" illustration found in my book *Rhythm*.) If we put the big rocks first into the jar of our schedule, we'll be able to fill in the cracks and gaps with pebbles. But if we put the pebbles in first, the big rocks likely will not fit.

What are the big rocks? Spiritual disciplines would be a big rock, that is for sure. But what about your distinct purpose? What has God called you to fulfill? Does it include writing? If so and you don't schedule it on your calendar as a "big rock first," you instead will allow pebbles to take preeminence and you'll struggle in fulfilling your writing goals. This example is just one among many.

The point is simple. Daily we face demands that can cause us to lose focus. Many distractions cross our path. Understanding and aligning with our why is the key to fulfilling our God-given desires.

Consider the following:

1. Write down your distinct why.

To do this, consider setting aside a day or two for prayer and deep reflection. Write down your dreams. This may include literal dreams from the Lord and dreams or visions (desires) you may have. Include prophetic words you may have received, especially if they are aligned with your calling, dreams, and visions. Last, include your gifting, talent, and abilities. The calling of God is not limited to your gift, but most often God will factor it in to your calling. Then considering such things, prayerfully write down your distinct purpose.

2. Write down your life's goals.

After accomplishing step one, step two should be easier to achieve than you might think. Don't get bogged down in trying to calculate your future accurately. That is not the point. The point is to consider all of the above items in step one. Based on such things, write out what you would like to accomplish throughout your life. Consider breaking it into five- or ten-year segments. It doesn't have to be expressed perfectly, and you don't have to show it to anyone else. It can be just between you and God.

3. Make life choices based on the above (unless God tells you something distinctly different).

Many times we become paralyzed by good opportunities. The key isn't filling our lives up with good things; the key is alignment with our why.

4. Help others walk a similar journey in discovering and aligning with their distinct why.

5. Consider ways in which you can lead ministry leaders to apply the above to specific ministries.

What is the why of a particular ministry? What are the five- and ten-year goals of the ministry? What decisions need to be made now that will best position us to fulfill those goals?

Conclusion

It doesn't take much thought to recognize the value and importance of aligning with our why. Too much of the church is caught up with trivial things, things that ultimately pale in comparison. It is the responsibility of spiritual leaders to help point the way, to influence others away from self-agenda toward God's agenda. Spiritual leaders do this by leading others to orbit around a worthy and compelling goal—the why.

ALIGNMENT

If you focus on performance instead of values, you will impress but will not impact.

In addition to leading others to center on the *why*, spiritual leaders also lead others to orbit around core values. Core values flow from philosophies or mind-sets and are exhibited in our behaviors. And it is one's behaviors that generate one's destination or result. Hence, core values matter a great deal.

As leaders our philosophies largely determine what we lead others to orbit around. If we believe God called us to grow the church, we value what helps the church grow. If we believe God called us to make disciples, we value what helps people grow. This is no slight matter.

As illustrated throughout the fable, the purpose of the fivefold ministry is to help others become mature disciples of Jesus Christ, to align with God's plan and purpose. It is not to lead the church to experience numerical growth; people must grow.

Jesus said, "I will build my church" (Matthew 16:18). Similarly, Paul taught that one plants, another waters, but God gives the increase (I Corinthians 3). Luke recorded that God added daily to the church such as should be saved (Acts 2:47). Other verses such as Matthew 28:19 and Ephesians 4:11–12 reveal the purpose of church leadership is not church growth. The primary purpose of church leadership is the growth of people. The good news is that changed lives result in church growth.

While keeping the most important thing at the forefront is important, we also can benefit from what the church growth movement can teach us. Things like the number of parking spots per a certain number of people (2.3 persons per parking spot) are beneficial, as is knowing that when you are at 70 percent of capacity, you should consider building or going to multiple services. Audio and video technology, service schedules and service transitions, systems, and so on also should be considered. But none are as important as growing people.

It is possible to invite others to the table, appreciate differences, address structure, and overcome self-interest by aligning with a worthy and compelling goal, and yet fail to equip (disciple) others. Misalignment is revealed in the placement of one's focus. When the focus is on performance, the desired result is that of church growth. We might believe performance will attract or perhaps keep people attending church, and by attending church, people will get saved or stay saved. So church growth (attendance) matters.

In contrast to church growth emphasis, value-centered church leaders focus on the growth of people. Believing that activity (attendance) does not equal spirituality, a value-oriented leader is centered on what grows a person. This is not to say that a value-centered church leader does not take part in activities and events or isn't concerned about attendance. It is simply to say that such things are not the center. The spiritual growth of people is the focus. That people engage in a journey of spiritual growth is of greater concern than the number of people who showed up at a service or an event. Moreover, church events and services have a central theme or purpose, which is the growth of people.

The lure of the performance-driven church is great. A high-quality performance is attractive. Who doesn't want to put their best foot forward? But is that the goal—to impress people? Or do we want to affect people? The answer is obvious. But perhaps we should ask yet another question: How do we best impact people? Is it through our performance or by being value driven?

While I would strongly argue that greater and lasting impact occurs through value-driven leadership, there is yet another reason to consider its benefits—personal longevity. The performance-driven approach most often leads to burnout. God did not call us to become performers; we are called to equip, to make disciples. God's grace is sufficient for what He has called us to do. It doesn't apply when we step outside of His plan and will for our lives. It is no wonder so many leaders struggle with health issues, relationship issues, and stick-to-itiveness; they have become overly concerned with the lesser thing. Like Martha, they need to choose the better thing.

What Are Core Values?

Core values are traits or qualities that represent an individual's or an organization's highest priorities. Core values are the things that really matter; they are the fundamental driving forces. They are the heart of who you are and what you do.

The power of identifying and aligning with core values is that it offers clear direction as to what you do or don't do. Core values also are known as guiding principles because they form a solid core of who you are and what you believe; how you act and react; who you are now and who you want to be going forward.

Core values serve as a magnet attracting others who share similar sentiments. They form the foundation of what occurs in the workplace. Core values help shape an organization's culture.

Becoming Value Driven

How does one center or orbit around values? What action steps should one take? Here are four things to consider:

1. Identify core values
2. Create virtue statements
3. Measure alignment
4. Uphold values

Identify Core Values

When identifying your core values, make sure you don't merely copy another church's core values. Identify your own. Every church is different; thus, it is likely that your core values will differ from another church's core values. For example, one church might place great emphasis on expressive worship, while another might place significant emphasis on teaching. The difference between the two churches can be seen in the congregation's behavior. The members of the church that emphasizes teaching might take significant notes on a notepad, whereas the members of the church that places great emphasis on expressive worship might gather in the front as soon as the congregation begins to sing. Most often, one does not see an equal amount of emphasis placed on both expressive worship and teaching that might involve members taking extensive notes. Neither church is more right than the other; they simply display different values. Again, your goal is to make sure you identify your core values, not another church's core values.

How do you identify your core values? First, ask yourself "What do we emphasize? What matters a great deal to us? What do we most often talk about? What do our behaviors reveal? In other words, if someone were to observe us for any length of time, what would they say about us? That church is a _____ church." Fill in the blank: a worshiping church? A giving church? A friendly church?

Consider asking your leadership team, "In order for us to be a growing, thriving Apostolic church, what key elements do we need?" Ask the team members to write a one- or two-word response per sticky note. This exercise should be completed in silence, each team member writing his or her personal thoughts.

After three to five minutes, have the team members place all sticky notes randomly on a wall. (Each team member should have ten or more sticky notes.) Then organize the sticky notes into like-minded groups. Typically with a group of ten to twelve people, there might be approximately 150 sticky notes. Once placed into like-minded groups, there might be eight core groups with some random leftover sticky notes.

After creating multiple core groupings, write them on a whiteboard or big sheet of paper. Look again for ways to merge. Are there groups that are similar? If so, can they be joined perhaps with a unique description or heading? Typically once the exercise is completed, you will have identified between three and five core elements to being the church you think you should be. These elements, for the most part, should be your core values.

The reason I have stated "for the most part" is because often one or more of the key elements isn't a true core value. Remember core values are revealed in behaviors. Identifying core values isn't about creating a wish list. Hence, while the above exercise is helpful in identifying core values, it also is beneficial in discovering that we may not be placing enough emphasis on some things we claim to be our core values. That leads to the importance of virtue statements.

Create Virtue Statements
Core values need to be reflected in virtue statements. Virtue statements help make core values come alive. They give definition as to what the core value is, what it means, and how it is lived out in real life.

One of the best ways to create virtue statements is to invite the team to create them. For example, if you have four core values, choose twelve leaders (it can be as many as you would like) and then divide into groups of four people (the optimal size is four to six people per group). Ask each group to craft three virtue statements. Depending on the number of leaders and the size of the groups, you might assign a particular core value to a specific group as opposed to all groups. If multiple groups are crafting virtue statements for the same core value, have the entire group select three of their favorite virtue statements.

Regardless of the specifics, the benefit of asking the team of church leaders to craft the virtue statements is that it helps solidify the core values in everyone's mind. One of the best ways to do this is to have them fill in the blanks: "Because we value _____, we will _____." By allowing them to have a voice, you are gaining buy-in. When everyone "owns" the core values, no one particular person has to "sell" the values to everyone else.

For example, if one of your core values is "serving," a virtue statement might be: "Because we value serving, we will look for opportunities to do the obvious without being asked to do so." Or "Because we value serving, we will volunteer one Saturday afternoon per month to assist an elderly person with household responsibilities."

The value or benefit of virtue statements is evident when the culture of the church reflects the statements. To this end, don't stop with creating virtue statements; expose the entire church to them. Weave them into messages and lessons. Invite others to share stories supporting the virtue statements. Use the virtue statements in promotional items, websites, and so on. Establish a culture that embodies the values you profess. All of this is done largely through the use of virtue statements.

Measure Alignment

One downside to identifying values is when leadership claims to hold certain values but then behaves contrary to the stated values. When this happens, motivation is deflated as followers lose trust in what leaders say.

Another downside to a focus on values is when a value-leak occurs. Value-leak occurs in a church when there is a lack of emphasis on a stated value. For example, a church might claim to value discipleship, but when months go by and there is little or no emphasis placed on it, what once might have been a value loses its value. In such cases, the stated value is hollow, and those in the church who do value discipleship lose heart and often look for a church elsewhere that does. Hence, measuring value alignment is important.

How does a church measure value alignment? One way is to create a safe place in which people are encouraged to speak up. Ask leaders to gauge how well the church is currently doing in areas pertaining to the stated values. View various departments, events, functions, and so on through the lens of your stated values. For example, if a stated value is serving, gauge the level of serving within the church. Look at the various functions of the church to see how well people are serving. If you are open to listening and not becoming defensive at what people might say, you can typically get a picture of how well the church is living up to its stated values. Again, the key is creating a safe environment.

Uphold Values

Not only is it important to talk about the stated values and invite and encourage others to do the same, appropriate action should be taken when the stated values have been violated. While you may not like confrontation, one of your responsibilities as a leader is to uphold your stated core values.

Upholding your values—protecting, building up, and supporting the stated values—requires you, as a leader, to lead the way. From time to time, this commitment may entail you getting involved in confronting someone(s) who has grossly violated those values. If so, you must do so in a way that supports the stated core values, not in a way that places you at the center. Your responsibility as a leader is not to protect yourself; it is to protect the stated core values. Your feelings should not take preeminence; the stated core values should be front and center. It isn't about a person or a personality; it is about your common purpose and core values.

A leader who is unwilling to demonstrate responsibility in upholding the stated core values will demotivate others, and they also will neglect to uphold core values. In contrast, leaders who will lead the way in modeling the stated core values and upholding them will create a culture throughout the church in which others will do the same.

Four Reasons You Need to Be Value Driven

A value-driven church is one in which the church culture exemplifies the stated values. In such a church, the core values transcend a value statement; they permeate everything the church does. The values lead the way. Such a church is truly value driven as opposed to performance driven.

There are many reasons you need to be value driven. Here are four:

1. Values help keep you centered on what is important.

It is easy to get sidetracked when leading a church. The abundant needs of people and the church can result in a leader spinning from one thing to another. At times it can be overwhelming and exhausting. The best way to lead, however, isn't one that destroys your health or relationships or leads to burnout. The best way to lead is to stay centered on what is most important, and that is the common purpose and core values. Therefore, one of the most important things you can do as a leader is to lead your team to discover and clearly state core values.

2. Values help you make sound decisions.

Values and decision-making are closely related. One drives the other. For example, an abundant array of opportunities can cause a leader to get sidetracked when making decisions. A value-driven leader, however, will find such times to be far less stressful because the values help lead the way in making a sound decision. When a leader knows what is most important, decision-making is easier to do. One of the benefits will be an increase in productivity in areas that matter the most. For example, a value-centered church may not offer an abundant number of ministries and events and programs, but its ministerial efforts are not inferior to a church that does. Quite the contrary. Its focus, its centeredness, causes it to excel. It knows what is most important and, as a result, makes sound decisions regarding its focus. As such, the church shines or stands out as leading the way. Such is a church that is value driven.

3. Values drive your daily actions and determine your destination.

When you have well-defined values and you maintain alignment with them, it will take you somewhere. Values drive behavior, and behavior determines your destination. If you don't like where you are or where you are headed, examine your values.

This is true both personally and collectively as a local church assembly. Values drive behavior, and behavior determines the destination. What one sows, one reaps. Such is the power of values.

4. Values keep you motivated.

Motivation is often a waning phenomenon; it comes and goes without one seemingly understanding what brought it in the first place or why it has seemingly left. But this is not so when one is value driven. Values keep you motivated as a person, and values keep a collective assembly motivated. When the stated values are aligned with the common purpose, everything flows more freely.

Trouble, however, will arise again. But being value driven will help keep you motivated and moving in the right direction. Knowing and aligning with the stated values will provide the motivation and momentum needed to sustain you, as well as the local church assembly, for the long haul. Such is the power of values.

Conclusion

Much can be said concerning values; this chapter simply touches on it. I strongly encourage you to dig deep into understanding values and what it means to be value driven. It is not a program. It is a lifestyle, a way of thinking that can transform your leadership and enhance the impact of the church in the world.

CONCLUDING THOUGHTS

The way a leader leads—the things he or she focuses on, the things done or not done—hold great ramifications regarding the organization's ability to achieve its objectives. In overcoming growth inhibitors, a church leader's level of leadership ability impacts the overall level of success. While there are additional factors and growth inhibitors, these fundamentals found in most North American churches are vital to growing people and, consequently, growing a church.

As shown throughout the fable and addressed in the application, leadership matters. Few would disagree. Yet many struggle to identify weaknesses within their own leadership ability. How do we overcome this?

Kurt Lewin, a physicist turned social scientist, described change as a three-stage process: unfreeze, change, and refreeze (further described in my book *Realign*). The analogy Lewin used involves a block of ice. How do you turn a block of ice into a reef in a punch bowl? Chisel it? Push and shove it? The answer is obvious. First, you must unfreeze it. Second, you must change its shape by placing it in a mold. Third, you must refreeze it. Thus, unfreeze, change, and refreeze. We become stuck when we cannot move from one stage to the next.

The beginning step to all positive change is self-awareness. Plainly stated, you will not change if you do not see your need for it. Therefore, self-awareness is a wonderful gift.

"In the year that king Uzziah died," wrote Isaiah, "I saw also the Lord sitting upon a throne, high and lifted up, and his train filled the temple" (Isaiah 6:1). Several points can be derived from this verse, but here is the one that stands out to me. It has to do with its connection to verse five: "Then said I, Woe is me! for I am undone; because I am a man of unclean lips, and I dwell in the midst of a people of unclean lips." Notice that when Isaiah saw the Lord, he acquired a more accurate view of himself: "Woe is me!"

An encounter with God can yield self-awareness. The Word of God, which is "sharper than any twoedged sword, piercing even to the dividing asunder of soul and spirit" (Hebrews 4:12), instructs and corrects us, helping us to see areas in which we need to change.

Additionally, the Lord uses other means to help us see areas in which we need to grow. Consider your spouse and family members. A spouse or other close family members likely know you better than anyone else. It pays to listen to what they might say regarding your leadership ability, which involves how you interact with others and how you might be perceived by those you lead. They will also point out your challenges and areas where you should grow.

Consider the voice of a close friend: "Faithful are the wounds of a friend; but the kisses of an enemy are deceitful" (Proverbs 27:6). Friends, however, will be shy in speaking what you need to hear if they don't feel safe enough to do so. The tragedy in the story of the emperor who wore no clothes is that, apparently, the emperor hadn't created a safe environment for his subjects to speak freely and truthfully.

For nearly twenty years I have routinely focused on a specific area of needed personal growth. For example, I have asked, "In what specific areas do I need to grow as a leader?" And "What do I need to change about my speaking to help me become a better speaker?" These are just two of several growth questions that I've asked close confidants for insight about things I might be lacking. The point is simple: The first step in growth is obtaining an awareness of a need for change. If we do not see our need to change, we will not unfreeze. We will not change.

The next step is to take responsibility for change. We must own the change. We cannot afford to make excuses. Sadly I've seen too many leaders come to some sort of realization of an area in which change is needed, only to resort to making excuses for the way things are. I get it. Change isn't easy. But I can't get to where I need to go without it. If I am going to grow, if I am going to change for the better, I must take responsibility. I must own it.

Third, if I am going to become the leader I need to be, a leader who overcomes growth inhibitors, I must focus on becoming God's version of me. My goal isn't to become something I'm not; my goal is to become the me God intends me to be.

Don't miss this: The purpose of change isn't to achieve our goals. It isn't to prove ourselves to other people or even to ourselves. That puts our glory at the center of change, and that is a sin. Christ must be the center. He is the reason we can help people grow, and that is how churches thrive.